THE
ONE-HOUR
BUSINESS
PLAN™

THE

ONE-HOUR BUSINESS PLAN™

THE SIMPLE AND PRACTICAL WAY
TO START ANYTHING NEW

JOHN McADAM

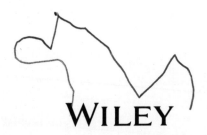

WILEY

Cover design: Wiley

Published by John Wiley & Sons, Inc., Hoboken, New Jersey.
Published simultaneously in Canada.

For general information about our other products and services, please contact our Customer Care Department within the United States at (800) 762-2974, outside the United States at (317) 572-3993 or fax (317) 572-4002.

Wiley publishes in a variety of print and electronic formats and by print-on-demand. Some material included with standard print versions of this book may not be included in e-books or in print-on-demand. If this book refers to media such as a CD or DVD that is not included in the version you purchased, you may download this material at http://booksupport.wiley.com. For more information about Wiley products, visit www.wiley.com.

Library of Congress Cataloging-in-Publication Data:

McAdam, John J.
  The one-hour business plan : the simple and practical way to start anything new / John McAdam.
     pages cm.
  Includes index.
  ISBN 978-1-118-72622-8 (cloth); ISBN 978-1-118-74715-5 (ebk)
ISBN 978-1-118-74714-8 (ebk)
1. New business enterprises-Planning. I. Title.
  HD62.5.M3863 2013
  658.1'1—dc23

                                              2013019138

Printed in the United States of America.

10 9 8 7 6 5 4 3 2 1

CONTENTS

Module 2

Who Are You Offering To?
The Customer Target Market

Module 3

Who Are Your Competitors?
Competitive Positioning

Module 4

Module 5

SETTING THE TONE

In this writing, I want to have a conversation with you as if we are meeting at a coffee shop, pub, or airport. This is not another BS business book where the author dumps from head to paper without facts or replicable tools for the reader. This work was strategically planned after years of experience and observations of more than 1,000 business plans and their results. What are the patterns and most essential elements of any business plan foundation? I write to share some answers with you here. I give you everything I have to date to support you with a foundation for your innovative journey. I've been educating innovators long enough to know that most of you will not write anything for myriad reasons, and I respect that. For those of you who do plan something in writing, welcome to the power of business planning and the benefits therein. At the end, if you share your written plan with us, we can collaborate on your journey and possibly make it safer and more enriching for you. The collective mind of our community is smarter and more experienced than I ever can or will be. Now, about our conversation . . .

INTRODUCTION

A One-Hour Business Plan foundation? Are you kidding me? Who can possibly write a business plan in one hour? It's impossible!

The "are you kidding me" I agree with. The "impossible," I simply do not—because it is the wrong answer. No, you cannot write a complete business plan in one hour. In fact, you should not, particularly if you are innovating something. After you take your innovation to market, and get feedback from your early customers, you will have to rewrite your business plan anyway, and who wants to do that? I love strategic business planning and I sure don't! My hope is to enable you to write a business plan foundation in an hour of writing (not thinking) time. Then you can write a more complete business plan after your customers have substantiated the value of your innovative offering, which will manifest via customer payments. Does this make sense yet?

If you still don't want to spend one hour writing a foundation plan for your business model, then think about this. More than 50 percent of businesses fail three years after their incorporation date. Why? The reasons are many. Experts, even our government, cannot agree on the final statistics for the reasons why business innovations fail. In fairness to the researchers, the question is difficult to answer because the reasons are myriad and we entrepreneurs tend to hide ourselves and move on after we fail. However, the research definitively shows a correlation of success to those businesses that had a business plan.

I have served approximately 1,000 business owners, CEOs, start-up businesses, and student entrepreneurs over the course of my career, including my own. I began counting them, but stopped because it made me feel old. However, I can conclude that a business with a strong business plan foundation is more likely to succeed than a business with a typical business plan. I know this from experience, and it is a self-evident truth for me. From my experience, the success versus failure seesaw tips toward success with the right business plan foundation, to the point where more than 50 percent of start-ups are still operating after three years. This observation is based on the hundreds of business plans that I have reviewed.

What good does it do my fellow human beings if I take this knowledge to my grave? Nothing! In this book, you find a blueprint for building a business plan foundation that is simple, strong, and enabling rather than complex, weak, and stifling. It is harder for me to write about the simple rather than the complex because intellectually I enjoy the complex more. On a personal note, for whatever reason, I take greater pleasure in watching my clients, students, and readers succeed than

I do in my own success. I take little pleasure in counting my money alone in a room. I am just not wired that way.

How do I write a business plan? What content should I include? The surgeon and the high-school dropout share this frustration. I know because I have taught them side by side. Their struggles are identical.

Therefore, my mission is to simplify what is clearly a daunting and complex task for most people (even actual rocket scientists), which is how to write a business plan. Not just any business plan, but a business plan foundation that can be written in one hour. This does not count the thinking time that you will need. You and I both know that you are thinking about your innovation frequently already, sometimes at very strange hours. We just have to focus together on the right thoughts. The right thoughts lead us to the right questions. The right thoughts and questions enable us to simplify a business planning process to its strongest foundation in the shortest amount of time.

I spent seven years searching for a method to help you write a business plan that will increase the likelihood of your success. Most of this time was spent arguing with myself about how to deliver this information. I started with the most complete business plan possible and ended with the most essential business plan components common to all. What a ride. I had to study my innovation failures more closely than my successes, as well as those of my clients, students, and friends.

The field-test results were embarrassing, in a good way. Nothing that I had ever done to date had been this good for so many people. At the risk of sounding paranoid, I know that my failure is coming in some form; I just don't know from where or when yet, my friend. Based on field-test results, the only failure that I see is the innovator's unwillingness to write anything. Some people prefer to stay in their dream state. The idea of converting their innovative thoughts to an actionable business plan evokes a fear, which stifles them and returns them to a more comfortable place (for them): their dream state of mind. I hope to help the dreamers get comfortable, and then realize their dream incrementally, iteratively, and with minimal risk.

As a side note, I have had the privilege of studying and teaching at arguably the finest and most innovative business school in the world. I did not write this book to impress my colleagues. I wrote it for you—to help you become more self-sufficient in earning money for yourself; to gently bring your great business idea down to earth and help you decide if you want to make that dream a reality.

I am not another rich guy writing a book about how I was successful and wanting to share it with you. I've seen that movie too many times. In fact, I publicly proclaim that I am a successful failure. These failures, while socially embarrassing and clinically depressing, I must admit, have strengthened me for innovative success with future innovations. Some of you may understand what I am talking about—and why I cherish failure.

One of the reasons I love strategic business planning so much is that I do not have to risk my life's savings anymore. I can experience that virtually—on paper, in simulation, and through dialogue with other people. Then I can do it again iteratively until I get it right on paper—and then and *only* then take it to market and make money. That is precisely what I show you how to do. I want to share a process, more than a format or a business plan structure. What you are about to see will appear oversimplified, but it is strong in its foundation. It is a business planning process that works. It is not 100 percent accurate; no business planning process can be. However, if you are willing to accept that we are only counting the writing time, not the thinking time, then you can write a business plan foundation in just one hour. (See Figure I.1.) Are you ready to get started?

It's been a ride

I guess I had to

Go to that place to get to this one

Now some of you

Might still be in that place

If you're tryin' to get out

Just follow me. I'll get you there.
—*Eminem, American rapper, record producer,
songwriter, and actor.* Recovery,
"Not Afraid"

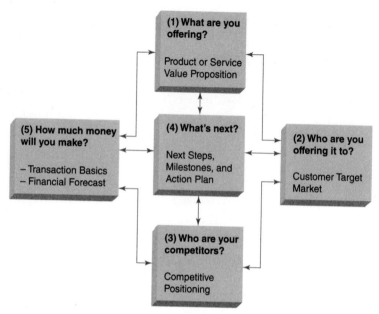

Figure I.1   The One-Hour Business Plan™ Foundation —Five Essential Business Plan Cornerstones

Before beginning, plan carefully.
—*Marcus T. Cicero, Roman Consul, senator, orator, philosopher, and constitutionalist. His work with European literature later initiated the fourteenth century Renaissance*

WHY THESE CORNERSTONES BUILD THE BEST FOUNDATION FOR ANY BUSINESS PLAN

Critics of the One-Hour Business Plan™ foundation might argue that other content is more important in building a foundation for a business plan. Perhaps other essential business plan components are more important such as the executive summary, mission statement, management team, or operations, to name a few. They might be right. However, they are missing the goal of the One-Hour Business Plan foundation process, which is to put the innovator in a unique position to test his or her offering, refine it based on customer feedback, then go to market more prepared for success. It makes more sense to write a complete business plan after the offering (product or service) is exchanged for value (money). This allows you to go to market with a customer-refined offering that is stronger, better prepared, and more likely to survive.

Allow me to share my rationale for including these five cornerstones as a business plan foundation by addressing the other most likely business plan cornerstone candidates. Let's start with the executive summary, which encompasses the highlights of a business plan, typically in one or two pages. Venture capitalists typically screen between 200 and 300 business plans to filter down to the one in which they will invest. Most often, they will read the executive summary first. If it is attention-grabbing, and meets their objectives (mainly around scaling profit quickly), then, the venture capitalists will read more. If not, the plan and opportunity are rejected (99 percent of the time). The executive summary is an important section. However, this business planning paradigm was created to make the early business model strong and help you refine the model or abort the venture, not to write a complete business plan. What I see as an instructor, advisor, and occasional investor when I read business plans are entrepreneurs writing the executive summary first, before writing the business plan—which is appalling to me. When you write the executive summary first, you ignore the broader purpose of the business planning process—to create a stronger enterprise before committing resources and going to market. Veteran business plan readers like me can tell when a business plan writer writes the executive summary first. They rarely stand up to the test of enterprise questioning. It's like watching a movie trailer and claiming that you saw the movie. It's like reading an abstract of a book and claiming you read the book. Who are you kidding? Write the executive summary last and save us all from this inevitable embarrassment.

Of all the other candidates available for business plan inclusion, the management team surfaces most resoundingly for me. My critics might disagree, but listen: a shrewd investor recognizes that the management team is arguably equally as important as the business model when deciding to invest. In a horse race, which is more important: the jockey or the horse? It's almost a rhetorical question. The fastest horse (an exceptional business model) will rarely win the race without the best jockey (the management team). The conversations I have with investors and the whispers I overhear during investor presentations about matching the management team with the business model are numerous. The entrepreneur is rarely aware that investors are questioning whether this team is the best jockey for their horse.

On a personal note, I have always been a thickly built male, in some areas thicker than I want to be (mainly in my head). Visualize the younger me, an American high-school football player or an adult rugby player who found nothing more relaxing than tackling people or being tackled. In the off-season, I lifted weights and ran alone on most days just to prepare for the upcoming season. Today, I practice yoga, in part to heal the residual pain from those glory days. Fast forwarding time, while raising our family in Chester County, Pennsylvania, I rode horses with my young son. One day, I decided that I wanted to run a horse and ride like the wind. I called the local horse farm and told them to get a fast horse ready for me because I was coming over to run—not to ride, but to run—and I was willing to pay. They had a horse ready for me when I arrived, all right, but they took one look at me, looked back at the horse, and brought the horse right back into the barn. The trainer told me to wait a minute and proceeded to bring out the largest, most muscular horse that I had ever seen. As an entrepreneur, what was my reaction? "I can handle this horse!" After the trainer saw us together for a while, walking, trotting, and galloping, she decided to turn us loose, alone. There were times during that ride when I thought I was going to die. There were other times when we were in such rhythm at full sprint that it felt like the horse was part of me and I was a part of it. The best piece of advice I ever received about horseback riding was to keep your heels down at all times. With my heels up and us at full stride, an unexpected mouse crossed our path and I nearly went over the horse's head.

If your business model is tested properly before launch, your business or new business initiative just might be similar to my favorite horseback ride: premature, out of control at times, wondering what is happening and how you got there. At other times you will be so in sync with your customers that time flies by, the value exchanges exhilarate you, and you will wonder how you ever lived happily without these exchanges taking place. However, all of that is premature at this time, in this context, with this customer target market (you). Yes, the management team (jockey) is critical. My point is that you can select the best jockeys for the horse later—after you learn more about your horse, the business model. You might think you know your horse now, but you need to walk, trot, and gallop with it first before you understand it more fully and turn the business model loose on your customer target market. Keep your heels down! How? We do this through various methods such as quality conversations, focused question and answer sessions, and getting valuable feedback about your offering.

Another candidate for the one-hour business plan foundation is operations. A well-described operating plan will explain how you will successfully deliver your product or service to your customer for a fair value. Wouldn't you rather write about your business operations after you make changes to your offering based on customer feedback? My conclusion is that the operations section should wait until after the offering becomes more clearly defined by the customer target market itself.

A quality mission statement is a beautiful sentence or paragraph that summarizes the purpose of the business model's existence. It encompasses the market, the contribution to that market, and what makes the offering unique or distinctive. Again, this is usually written first, but it *should* be written later, after customers tell you what makes you distinctive, unique, and economically competitive in your market. Although it would be the easiest module to cover in 10 minutes, we will table it for now, not because it is less important, but because your operations plan will change significantly after early customer feedback and after going to market successfully.

Pardon my tangential digressions. I am justifying the inclusion of these five modules as the most important components for a business plan foundation. Anything else will unnecessarily compete for your time and energy when you are innovating something new or writing a business plan. Hopefully you agree, or at least respect my efforts to preserve your resources, mainly time, energy, and money. Let's begin.

Price is what you pay. Value is what you get.
—*Warren Buffett, American investment
entrepreneur and philanthropist*

MODULE 1

---

*What Are You
Offering?*

Create a Value Proposition
That Makes a Stronger
Business Model

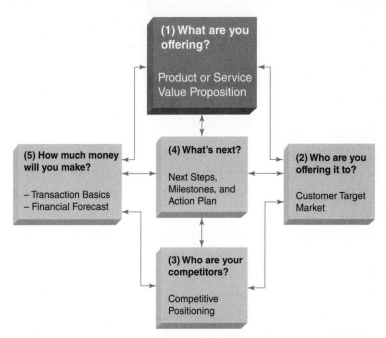

Figure 1.1   The One-Hour Business Plan™ Foundation —Five Essential Business Plan Cornerstones

Investopedia defines a value proposition as "a business or marketing statement that summarizes why a consumer should buy a product or use a service. This statement should convince a potential consumer that one particular product or service will add more value or better solve a problem than other similar offerings." (See Figure 1.1.)

The word *consumer* in the definition is inherently interchangeable with *business* to accommodate both business and consumer purchases. The second sentence in the definition defines the foundation and the reason consumers or businesses purchase specific goods and services—to add value or solve problems better than other available offerings. If the statement convinces the purchaser that value is added or a problem is solved, then the purchase benefits both buyer and seller and a transaction should naturally occur. Well done, *Investopedia*!

In summary, the value proposition defines what the organization does and its purpose for being—to add value and benefit the purchaser. Unfortunately, articulating a value proposition is a challenge for most of us. You might think that larger organizations articulate their value propositions better than smaller organizations. Not in my experience. As a test, if you want to embarrass the CEO of a large organization, take a tape recorder to random employees and managers in the organization and ask, "What does this organization do?" Play the recorded answers back for the CEO and watch the facial expressions unfold. Fun stuff if the CEO has a sense of humor; otherwise, not so much. In fairness to the CEO, it is challenging to consistently communicate a business value proposition that is easily understood and replicable to all levels of an organization. If the employees don't know, imagine how the customers of the organization feel at times.

Do you think it is harder or easier for the start-up entrepreneur to answer the question, "What does your organization do?" I find it fascinating that both

CEO and entrepreneur tend to struggle similarly while answering this question. When the value proposition is unclear in a businessperson's mind, this person tends to over-explain it in feature-oriented details and in ways that make it difficult for the listener to understand the value being exchanged or to even pay attention. A lengthy or unclear value proposition reminds me of sports fans who listen to their spouse talk about shopping while the playoff game is on television in the background (I have heard). It is difficult to focus and lay the foundation for a natural business transaction without an effective value proposition.

The value proposition of the business model is the starting point for the business plan. It provides a basic framework to clarify the answer to the question, "What do you do?" Because you want the customer to buy what you are selling, imagine that you are the customer making the buying decision. What do you need to know to decide whether to buy the offering? To build the foundation for the value proposition, we answer some fundamental questions, and then add brevity and clarity to record the value proposition for the first phase of the One-Hour Business Plan foundation.

THE NEED

What is the *need* being filled? What void does your product or service fill that is not currently being satisfied adequately for customers?

Wherever a man turns, he can find someone
who needs him.
—*Albert Schweitzer, German, then French,
theologian, philosopher, and medical missionary;
Nobel Peace Prize 1952*

An entrepreneur is born when an unmet need is identified, a solution is created, successful marketing processes are established, and customers pay for the solution (and the check clears). The customer valuing the solution substantiates the need, the value proposition, and the business model. Veteran entrepreneurs understand that paying customers mean everything to the new venture. They seek quicker and more cost-effective ways to get the value proposition in front of the customer target market for feedback, evaluation, and purchasing decisions.

The caveat for the entrepreneur is to avoid perceiving a need that the customer does not value. You must avoid the "a solution looking for a problem" syndrome. In other words, the entrepreneur believes there is an obvious need, while the customer does not care enough about the problem to value the offered solution. To avoid this syndrome, the existence of a need matching a valuable customer solution must be created, tested, and refined before significant time and resources are deployed to offer it to more target customers. Otherwise you will waste time, energy, and money.

In terms of business planning, establishing the need starts laying the foundation for creating the value proposition. The entrepreneur can answer some fundamental questions to document the need. What is not happening in the target market today that should be happening? What potential customers have you spoken with about these needs and your solution? What was the feedback? Where is the void in the solutions being offered by competitors and competitive substitutes? (More on competition later.) Ask yourself questions like these to achieve this first cornerstone and begin the foundation for the value proposition.

The need for solutions exists in a variety of forms. There might be better solutions available, not only in the benefits provided by the product or service itself, but also in how the solution is marketed, packaged, priced, serviced, geographically focused, and so on. For example, the world might not have needed a cola beverage, or even another cola beverage, but an improved cola beverage was created. How? Perhaps there was a need for a larger variety of beverage offerings in food service institutions. A consumer was thirsty while away from home and a water fountain was not available; a store or food service establishment was not open. How were these needs identified and established?

Mental Exercise: The Need

Think about how customers in your target industry interact. What events, behaviors, and conditions lead up to the need for your product or service? Ultimately, what need does your product or service fill? Verbalize the need out loud. Does it sound meaningful for potential customers? Restate the need, this time making it both clearer and more precise.

THE SOLUTION

> Business must be the solution, not the problem.
> —*Dennis Weaver, American actor*
> *in the television series* Gunsmoke

We American entrepreneurs have a tendency to spend a disproportionate amount of time working on the solution before we fully understand the problem or explain it clearly as a need. The need must be clearly and concisely identified before you start working on the solution; otherwise, you start to solve the wrong problem. Therefore, if you have not clarified the need in the marketplace by now, go back to the prior section and explain the customer need before continuing.

The solution should be the easy part of building the value proposition. The solution is something we create for others and find innovative ways to call the creation our own.

With the need of the customer in mind, our next step is to articulate the importance of the solution to the customer. Be forewarned and mindful that during the solution development process we all have a tendency to follow the path of least resistance.

The solution our target customers want might not be the one that we have the most fun creating, or be the easiest, or the most cost-effective for us to deliver. Our work experiences might unnecessarily limit our creative thinking toward a solution. For example, a software programmer experienced in developing software for mobile phone applications who has identified a need in computer games might not have software development experience in the gaming market to come up with a solution.

Here, the engineer might have a tendency to use the mobile programming solutions for mobile applications he already knows well, which might not be the best programming solutions for the gaming customer. New solutions might be needed in a different programming language for unique gaming hardware. Just be mindful of our human tendency to revert back to what we feel comfortable with and what we know and understand. Our eye should be on the prize—the customer. Better still, we must be looking through the customer's eyes. Stand directly behind your prospective customer and stay there. What do you see?

A quality entrepreneurial solution begins objectively, with the customer's needs in mind. Remember the need section? We are thinking about how our target customers interact and the problems they encounter, which creates opportunities for solutions. What is the solution for the need that solves a fundamental problem for your target customer? Sticking with the cola beverage example, various product needs were filled over time by packaging the beverage in various sizes of containers as well as for soda fountains. Vending machines were built and dedicated to delivering the beverage even when stores or food service institutions were closed. New solutions evolved.

Mental Exercise: The Solution

Think about your solution now and verbalize it out loud. Repeat it for brevity and clarity in a way that people outside the industry can understand.

FEATURES VERSUS BENEFITS

Features

> Normal people . . . believe that if it ain't broke,
> don't fix it. Engineers believe that if it ain't
> broke, it doesn't have enough features yet.
> —*Scott Adams, American creator*
> *of the* Dilbert *comic strip*

The features of the offering are important for the customer to understand. They are tangible descriptions of the product or service that can be seen and touched. The business owner and its employees are the most familiar with its features, because they work with those features each day when delivering and servicing the offering. The features describe the offering objectively. Some customers study features in an effort to compare one offering to another. Therefore, the distinguishing and original attributes of the features are the most important to describe as they enable an offering to stand out in a crowded marketplace.

Examples of features commonly seen in commercial advertising include:

- Larger screen size
- Open 24 hours
- 100 speed-dial settings
- Custom purchase programs
- Bulk packaging

These features are factual statements about the product or service offered. How does the customer respond to these features? Customers are more interested in what the offer does for *them* than they are in what the offering does. As consumers, we often ask ourselves, "What do I get from this?" To highlight what the offering does for the customer, the benefits need to be explained.

Benefits

He who lives only to benefit himself confers on the world a benefit when he dies.

—*Tertullian, Latin Christian author from the Roman province of Africa; best known for advancing the term Trinity*

The benefits of the product or service offering are intangible benefits, which transfer to the customer through the value exchange. Benefits are experiences that the customer values as a result of utilizing the product or service.

What is the difference between a feature and a benefit? A feature is tangible while a benefit is intangible. A feature describes what the service or the product does. A benefit portrays what the customer gets. For example, the features of a cola soft drink include the package design, the taste distinctions, the carbonation level, and physical appearance. The benefits of the cola beverage include a quenched thirst, social acceptance of your beverage choice, a cost savings, convenience of use, and prestige, among others.

Another way to view benefits is to explain them as natural extensions of features that the customer enjoys. For example, the benefits associated with the aforementioned list of features might include:

- A larger screen size on a cellular phone saves me time squinting and slowing down to read text as I must do with smaller screen sizes. I will also be less annoyed trying to view small text.

- A grocery store open 24 hours a day provides convenience for me to shop when my schedule permits or during emergencies.

- Having 100 speed-dial settings on an office telephone allows me to keep in touch with almost everyone I might call, by using one step rather than multiple steps. This saves me time.

- Custom purchase programs save me money by allowing me to purchase only what I need, not more than I want or will use.

- Bulk packaging saves me money by purchasing less packaging and labor without compromising quality.

If you are a customer, are you more interested in a feature or a benefit? Benefits rule! Benefits are what the customer gets. A benefit created by empathetically viewing your prospective customer's needs generates value. Be mindful of our natural tendency to describe features, since it is relatively easier. Therefore, focus on the benefits to create your distinguished value proposition for your customer.

Mental Exercise: Features and Benefits

Think about the tangible features of the product or service and verbalize them out loud. Mentally list the benefits (often intangible) that the customers receive by utilizing your product or service. What is in it for them? What are the most important benefits that your customer receives?

Take advantage of the ambiguity in the world.
Look at something and think what else it
might be.

—*Roger von Oech, American speaker, conference
organizer, author, and toy-maker, whose focus has
been on the study of creativity*

ADVANTAGES

To describe the advantages of a value proposition offering
we need to get inside our customers' heads and predict
how they will view the purchasing decision after understanding our value proposition. A customer normally
has multiple choices to make when purchasing among
competitors or competitive substitutes. Competitive substitutes are products or services that can be purchased
that might not be close to what you are offering, but are
solutions that fill the need or solve the problem in the
customer's opinion. Therefore, they are significant and
must be considered as we draft the value proposition. We
go more into depth with competitors and competitive
substitutes when we get to that critical section. Here,
we simply need a basic understanding of the competitive dynamic in the marketplace so we can preliminarily
predict who might be closest to our value proposition
offering.

First let us avoid the second biggest lie in the world
and one of the greatest lies in business: "I have no competition." Admittedly, it is possible for a value proposition

to have no competition, but it is a rare instance. Rarer still is a value proposition that has no competitive substitutes. Don't let your acknowledgment of competitive substitutes deter you, but inform you. If you ignore your competition now, you will have to account for competition later during the sales process when a customer informs you who or what they purchased rather than your offering. When developing a quality value proposition, we must, at a high level, account for competition or competitive substitutes.

Before moving on to the mental exercise for the advantages of a value proposition, let's consider an example. Suppose that you own an independent bookstore in the suburbs. A friend recommends a book to one of your potential customers. What are the decisions that your customer will make before purchasing the book? Some background: the customer prefers to own the book because his friend references it in group conversations. He would like to sample the book before buying, and prefers used books. Also, there might be a discussion of the book at a group meeting next week. Four samples of competitive choices where the customer can purchase the book include:

1. An online store such as Amazon.com, with new and used options.

2. A bookstore chain.

3. An independent bookstore.

4. The library.

What are the advantages of each of these four competitive choices for the customer?

1. An online store enables the customer to **order** the book new or used **quickly**, but the customer must wait until next week to receive it or pay for expedited shipping. Used book **prices** might be lowest here.

2. A bookstore chain has a **suburban location, new books**, and a **wide selection**, but might not have the book because it has been out of print for a few years.

3. The independent bookstore is located in an **urban area** close to many work locations and has **spacious reading areas** to browse books before purchasing. A well-read and **knowledgeable staff** has read most of the books in the store. A wide **used book selection** provides the customer the opportunity to sample the condition of the book before purchasing.

4. The library may not have the book, but can acquire it in a few days; however, the book must be returned.

Which of these do you include in your value proposition as an independent bookstore owner? The online bookstore is soulless; removed from the equation are people with whom customers can speak. A knowledgeable, well-read staff sounds like a competitive advantage here.

Bookstore chains do not carry used books for a number of reasons. A used book offering sounds like another competitive advantage. I mention the library as an example of a competitive substitute that must be recognized, because customers often consider competitive substitutes in their purchasing decision. Therefore, they should be accounted for in the independent bookstore's value proposition.

Mental Exercise: The Advantages

Who are the top competitors for your product or service? At a high level, what advantages does your value proposition possess over those competitors?

Think about these advantages objectively, like an industry analyst, without emotional attachment. We include them in the value proposition.

To stay on schedule for The One-Hour Business Plan, you have 10 minutes to write down your value proposition before moving on to the next module. Mental preparation in the form of building the foundation and taking notes does not count against your time. You are on the clock when you start writing the value proposition and then refine it for brevity, clarity, and customer focus. Most of us find it easier to read and think than we do to write. To challenge you and make it a game, the clock starts ticking when you start writing to complete the value proposition worksheet.

Before we get to the value proposition exercise, I want to share a story with you about a value proposition.

In one of my strategic business planning classes, there was a husband-and-wife team who delivered the following approximate value proposition to the class: "Pickled Willy's offers premium pickled seafood (crab tails, halibut, and cod) from a family recipe through high-end retail stores, distributors, and directly to consumers (via the Internet) from Alaska." The reaction from the class caught me off guard. This adult class of business professionals began making fun of the value proposition.

Pickled Willy's was a start-up business at the time. I attempted to teach the group not to judge a business model prematurely and that management team members who write business plans are often more successful than individuals who write them. I got through to some, but most people in the room just could not believe that such a value proposition would be successful. "Who wants pickled seafood?" I overheard. I am contractually precluded from sharing with you how many or which business models were successful from that group of entrepreneurs and business owners. I do have permission to tell you about Pickled Willy's. Barbara, the wife, set up a second residence in Kodiak, Alaska, without her husband, to start up a seafood processing and distribution facility with her Uncle Willy. That alone takes some pickled balls! She has an Alaskan work ethic that makes the rest of us look lazy. Pickled Willy's took off. Her list of customers and her distribution reach continue to generate envy from the competitor substitutes in her industry. She calls me once in a while to remind me how well she is crushing the financial objectives I helped her put together (she, like many, despises forecasting metrics) and laughs with competitive pleasure. I never told her that I sandbagged them for her (more on sandbagging later).

I share this story with you here to help you prepare mentally to write your distinctive value proposition relative to your competition without judgment and as an inspiration to focus. Focus on the customer's needs and on what's missing. Identify the distinctive descriptor(s) of benefits that encompass your vision, make the offering compelling, make the customers want to learn more, and take the next step of a sales transaction. Imagine the key benefit that grabs the attention of the skeptical customers and even generates debate. Look at your customers and offer what they will be curious enough to try!

WRITTEN EXERCISE: WRITE YOUR VALUE PROPOSITION

Write a value proposition based on the solution offered in terms of benefits to your customers relative to primary competition. You have no more than 10 minutes to complete the exercise, so set a timer or alarm and get started.

The value proposition should be delivered verbally in approximately 15 seconds, which is about the attention span of the typical person who asks you, "What do you do?" In written form, it should be between two and four sentences in length. Most writers would agree that it takes longer to write with brevity and clarity than just to write. Your task here is to write briefly and clearly while including the core elements of a quality value proposition: need, solution, feature, advantage, and benefit. They should not be separate sentences, but should blend together naturally. I suggest getting the first draft out and editing afterward.

VALUE PROPOSITION EXERCISE #1—THE VALUE PROPOSITION BUILDING BLOCKS

In this exercise (Figure 1.2), we bring the five building blocks together with intentionally limited spacing. As you create, write comparatively more about the need and the benefits than the features or solutions.

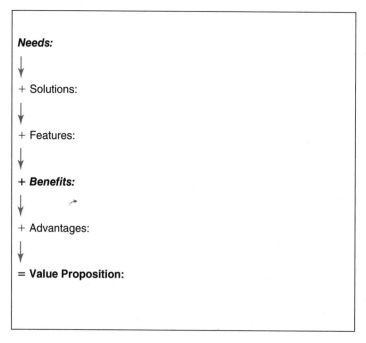

Figure 1.2   The Value Proposition Building Blocks

Self-Quality Control Check for Module 1: The Value Proposition

- Does your value proposition mention the need for the offering?

- Does the solution focus on benefits for the customer? Are the benefits natural extensions of the features?

- Are the advantages to primary competitors expressed distinctively?

- Is the value proposition brief, clear, and understandable to someone outside the industry?

- Is this value proposition deliverable in 15 seconds during the course of normal business conversation?

We have to get your value proposition as clear, distinctive, beneficial, and intriguing as we can before we move on. Again, if the value proposition fails to express the benefits of what the recipient gets, then the rest of our business plan and business model will suffer greatly. We are not ready to move on yet. Value Proposition Worksheet #1 summarizes what professors teach us in marketing classes in business schools. It might not work for you in your industry in the sound-bite society we live in today. The blunt truth is that businesspeople rarely give a damn about your features or how you do what you do. Sometimes they don't even care about what you do. What most businesspeople want to know is what is in it for them! What do they get? Value Proposition Exercise #2 is designed to be your default value proposition to communicate to your listener exactly what your customer gets and experiences by working with you.

VALUE PROPOSITION EXERCISE #2—"WHAT DO YOU DO?"

This can be your value proposition when you are tired after a long day and must deliver it quickly. In this exercise, we simply focus on the need and how the customer benefits from the offering. See Figure 1.3.

Someone asks you, "What do you do?"
You might want to answer that question in two sentences. Therefore, complete these two statements by filling in the blanks:

We work with people who need _____.

This benefits them by_____.

Figure 1.3   What Do You Do?

Five Tips for Quality Control

1. Are you delivering it verbally in 15 to 30 seconds?

2. Do you have any "and" clauses? If so, you are probably rambling on and your listener is starting

to glaze over you. Force yourself to remove these clauses.

3. Are you communicating from your customer's perspective and not yours?

4. Have you committed your value proposition to memory so you don't have to read it? That's how it works in the real world.

5. Deliver this verbally to multiple people and ask for feedback.

Field-test results reveal that some of you will still be stuck after completing the first two value proposition exercises. You might not even know it. Some of us flat out struggle to find empathy with our customers. If your value proposition merely states what you do and how you do it, then I need you to work on your why. Why do you do what you do?

One of the most successful authors of all time is Jack Canfield, author of the *Chicken Soup for the Soul* series of books. *Chicken Soup for the Soul* books help us to heal ourselves when we need it. The value proposition is actually in the title. How many books do you think that Jack Canfield sold with his co-author Mark Victor Hansen? 50,000? 500,000? 5 million? The answer is more than 500 million books. Jack and Mark achieved this level of success for a number of reasons, but one of them is because the value proposition was communicated to the reader in the title of the book—to a wide, addressable customer target market.

Jack is in a different place now. His company, Strategies for Success, at www.jackcanfield.com, provides tools, tips, and resources to find your why, articulate your vision, and take action toward your definition of success. At first, it might sound like enthusiasm without substance, which is in vain. It is not. Some of us simply are stuck and need to loosen up, lighten up, and look upward. The exercises come in handy, particularly when we are stuck.

For example, I had the privilege of meeting Jack Canfield at a writer's conference. Prior to our brief meeting he taught us writers a breakout group exercise called "What do you want?" Here we broke into pairs of two, one questioner and one responder. The questioner asks, "What do you want?" repeatedly. The responders are free to answer that question any way they desire. We all have different wants for ourselves, our family, our business, our career, or simply in the moment. The key for the responder is to answer each question honestly about whatever thought comes to mind.

VALUE PROPOSITION EXERCISE #3—"WHAT DO YOU WANT?"

The purpose of this exercise is to find your purpose by repeatedly answering variations of the question with openness, tolerance, acceptance, passion, and a sense of humor.

See Figure 1.4 for the "What do you want?" exercise.

The questioner asks you, "What do you want?" repeatedly. Perhaps (but it is not required) the Questioner adjusts the question a bit by asking, "Why do you want that?" or "What do you want to accomplish with that?"

Answer the question: "What do you want?" repeatedly and as many times as you can in five minutes!

What do you want? _____.

What do you want? _____.

What do you want for you? _____.

What do you want for your family?_____.

What do you want for your business? _____.

Figure 1.4 What Do You Want?

Spend a lot of time talking to customers face to face. You'd be amazed how many companies don't listen to their customers.

—Ross Perot, American presidential candidate and founder of Electronic Data Systems

Who Are You Offering To? The Customer Target Market

The Only Sustainable Source of Business Funding for the Long Term

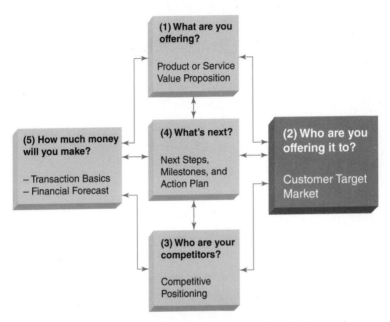

Figure 2.1   The One-Hour Business Plan™ Foundation —Five Essential Business Plan Cornerstones

Consumers are statistics. Customers are people.
—*Stanley Marcus, former Chairman of luxury retailer Neiman Marcus*

CUSTOMER TARGET MARKET INTRODUCTION

An innovation needs to be attached to a customer. Without sufficient customers at a specific value, nothing else matters. Some of the most comprehensive detailed business plans I have seen identified a market only to find the market in question insufficient to sustain the business model. The reason the customer target market module comes next (see Figure 2.1) is to help you assess whether your offering has sufficient value for customers by testing it with them first. This justifies the economic purpose of most business models, which is to make money.

In this module, we go through a series of steps to help you develop an initial customer list to approach to get answers to such critical questions as: How much are they willing to pay? How often do they purchase in a year? What is the sales cycle time? The size of a target market is challenging to determine, because government classification systems are often too broad to benefit the entrepreneur, and firms that pay for private research do not share results for obvious reasons. The point is to make sure that your target market is not too small or too limited to support the business model that you are trying to build. Make a logical estimate based on a foundation of rational facts, and decide if you can live with the estimate of the addressable market size.

At the end of this module, you should produce an initial list of customers to approach, or the module is for naught. You will be able to describe your target customer market in terms of a demographic profile, which will help you reach more prospective customers. Based on my experience, the second-phase customers are the hardest to generate, because marketing methods have not been fully refined or even implemented yet. Second-phase customers are defined as customers who purchase an offering after the first phase of customers purchase through various marketing methods.

Conversations with customers, held early and often, are extremely critical for a new venture or product launch. Time flies by when you are speaking to prospective customers. What are the most essential questions that you need to ask people or companies that might be your customer? The trick is to focus on the most important critical assumptions about the business model, which commonly include the price they are willing to pay, top benefits desired, top features wanted, purchasing frequency, substitute products or services, and buying decision time, among others.

Forget about writing five business plan modules in an hour for a moment. If you can only do one thing—and one thing only, regarding business planning—it should be to get feedback on your value proposition from your future customers before you get too invested financially. As an entrepreneurial axiom, the business model looks very different before revenue than it does postrevenue, so why start anywhere other than with your customer?

MARKET SIZE: THE ADDRESSABLE MARKET

Many business planners spend too much time explaining the target market from a qualitative or statistical perspective when we need to focus on individual transactions. However, understanding the market overall helps you to know the individual purchasers better, which brings you closer to a transaction. You don't want to enter a market and learn that it only has 109 potential customers (like I once did). Therefore, you should have a quantitative understanding of your total customer target market. You probably will not be able to describe your target market accurately in one number, but having an acceptable range of numbers for the addressable customer target market is more than sufficient.

At this point the entrepreneur often looks at me and asks, "Where the hell do I get that information?" Examples of potential sources of quantifying your target market include: trade associations (the good ones know), industry databases, private research, trade publications, list brokers, Internet sources such as Reference USA, Dun & Bradstreet's *Million Dollar Database*, Hoover's Online, or a business-school library's reference desk. Many other sources exist, particularly online, to help you quantify your addressable market.

Avoid defining your addressable customer target market only using the XYZ method, defined here as X percent of the customers with Y demographics in Z industry. I can't take it anymore! One of my favorite business authors, Guy Kawasaki, finally snapped with frustration over entrepreneurs defining their addressable market in this way and wrote *The Art of the Start*. Here, part of what Guy teaches us is how to address the customer target market from the transaction up, and aggregate those transactions, as opposed to working from the top down using the XYZ method. Thanks, Guy!

Note that I am not asking you to avoid quantifying your target market. In fact, that is the next section. My point is to use both the XYZ method and the customer transaction method of defining your addressable market from the top down and bottom up respectively. Then, the market size should be more addressable as top-down and bottom-up methods begin to reconcile to prepare you for your business journey. Your business plan will be more useful in your daily, weekly, monthly, quarterly, and annual activities as you seek to acquire additional customers. That said, let's attempt to describe and quantify your customer target market next.

Customer Demographics and Demographic Profiles

Customer demographics are objective descriptors of a population. When searched in a large database, the demographics serve as criteria to narrow down the database to a quantifiable number. Try this after completing the One-Hour Business Plan foundation in writing when you need to identify additional target market customers.

After listing the customer demographics, combine them to form a demographic profile. A demographic profile provides enough information about a typical group member to create a mental picture of the group for target marketing purposes. This mental picture helps you choose the marketing methods most likely to reach your customer target market for responses, which become sales leads for follow-up to convert into customers.

An example of an addressable customer target market description is a business-to-business (B2B) marketer for website ecommerce targeting business owners with more than $100,000 in revenue and five or more employees in the business-to-consumer (B2C) industry, with an existing website and within a 100-mile radius of Houston, Texas. A list of these prospective target market customers can be acquired through the aforementioned sources and others. Afterward, you will not only have the approximate number of customers in this market, but also their contact information to market to them.

CUSTOMER CATEGORIES

Customer categories are groups of customers with common purchases. For established businesses, it helps to know existing and prospective customer categories for target marketing and avoiding marketing to customers who do not purchase the category being marketed. For new business ventures, it is insufficient to only list and describe customer categories as the target market, if the entrepreneur stops there. Categories by themselves are too broad to market to. Names and contact information are paramount. I have seen too many entrepreneurs describe their customer target market in terms of categories only, and then not market to them. If you have little time or energy, create a mental picture of your demographic profile for the customer target market and simply create a list of people who fit that profile to offer your value proposition to. This is the written exercise at the end of this module.

SECOND-PHASE CUSTOMERS

The initial list of prospective customers who might purchase your offering should not be too difficult to find. You created your business idea with people or businesses in mind that might purchase the concept. However, it is the second list or second phase of customers that entrepreneurs seem to struggle with the most—perhaps because second-phase customers are inherently unknown and must be acquired through marketing. I observe this struggle both as an entrepreneurial practitioner and as a business advisor. I do not have empirical research to support the claim, but I intuitively and experientially know that second-stage customers are a common new-venture problem to manage and need special attention in the form of target marketing management. Let's address that next.

THE CUSTOMER TARGET MARKET FUNNEL

"How do I find more customers?" I am asked this question by companies doing hundreds of millions of dollars, middle-market business owners, and start-up entrepreneurs alike. It is something we all have in common as businesspeople. It is a question we need to keep asking ourselves frequently, or our businesses will ultimately contract. Only the fortunate few are unconcerned about where new customers will come from. They are probably not reading this and are not too concerned about business planning. However, business cycles ultimately include new competitive changes, product and service replacements, maturation, and changing customer demands, which ultimately lead to the need for additional customers.

Here, we explore various methods for sales, marketing, advertising, and public relations, which support the inevitable effort of finding new customers. The goal is to get you thinking in new ways about how to draw in and reach out to the next customer for your business. The classification of the four categories might be debatable, but don't get hung up on that. For example, some methods, like networking and referrals, clearly fall into both sales and marketing.

To support this principle visually, I think of the four methods of reaching customers as a funnel that circulates and recycles again and again. The mouth of the funnel, with the widest part of the opening can be compared to public relations, which often has the broadest reach around the customer target market. Compare advertising with the next phase of the funnel that narrows down the customer target market even more by getting closer to your customer. The funnel bandwidth of advertising qualifies your customer target market with plenty of nonpotential customers, but not as many as public relations. The third stage of the funnel—marketing—gets closer still to the customer by specifically narrowing the customer target market by reaching mostly those who might be interested in the offering. The final stage of the funnel—sales—now puts you in front of the decision makers who at some level are interested in your business offering. Sales commitments (revenue for you) should ultimately come out of the narrow end of the funnel. Stick with me here, because this is not your typical funnel in a literal sense. It recirculates; it leaks out both ends and into the other sections of the funnel, unpredictably at times. For fluid transfer, this funnel would drive you crazy. For finding new customers, it becomes energizing, enriching, and even fascinating when potential "customer fluid" starts interacting with other funnel phases, recycling itself and evolving into a new customer machine. I can't leave this section without at least drawing a picture for you. See Figure 2.2.

What does your funnel look like? Let's build the customer target market funnel from four basic parts, from the widest audience reach to the narrowest focus via public relations, advertising, marketing, and sales. We define the terms, present a menu of choices as if you were in a restaurant, and have you choose one method to build your funnel for second-stage customers.

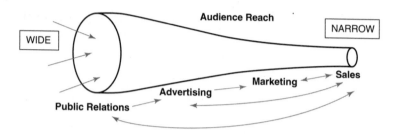

Figure 2.2   The Customer Target Market Funnel

PUBLIC RELATIONS

> Some are born great, some achieve greatness,
> and some hire public relations officers.
> —*Daniel J. Boorstin, American historian,
> professor, attorney, and writer; 12th Librarian
> of the United States Congress*

The core role of public relations (PR) is to craft and maintain the corporation's image. The hunger for quality content from all forms of media—while historically utilized by larger organizations—plus rapidly developing PR Internet tools, in conjunction with the need to reach more potential customers, has unleashed the benefits of PR for small business owners. For our purpose here, we look at PR as a method to develop market awareness (in a broad sense) for your value proposition.

Think about PR in ways that benefit the triad of people or entities involved in the process: you, the media, and the reader/listener/viewer collectively. If you overlook or ignore the needs of one of the PR triangle members, then the PR process breaks down and the subsequent results will most likely disappoint you. What do the media want from its content? Anybody? They want to sell more advertising. How do they sell more advertising? Media sells more advertising by attracting more readers, viewers, and listeners and by informing potential advertisers. Quality content alone is of little value to the media if the content does not increase the number of readers, viewers, or listeners. If you choose a PR method, remember the PR triangle (pictured in Figure 2.3) and account for the needs of each participant before releasing PR materials.

Sharing how to craft better PR is outside the scope of this book. However, as a rule of thumb, remember

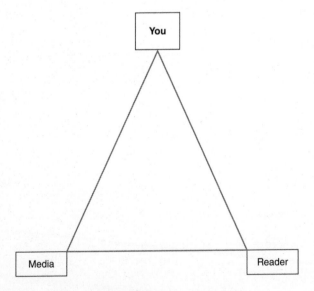

Figure 2.3   The Public Relations Triangle

to promote the benefits (what the reader gets), not the features, of your value proposition from Module 1. Always suggest the next step for your potential customer in any PR document so you can track responses. After all, the responses are the fun part of PR—they are the harvest from your customer-farming labor.

Here is a short list of PR methods commonly available for businesses. If you employ others that are effective at creating responses, let me know so that I might share those methods with others in need of PR. For now, choose one of these methods or another to build awareness for your value proposition.

Mental Exercise: Choose a Public Relations Method

You are sitting in a business restaurant; I am your waiter and have just handed you a menu of the PR choices that follow. Which PR methods are you and your potential customers most comfortable with?

- Press releases—electronic and print
- Speaking engagements
- Community sponsorship
- Nonprofit board membership
- Volunteer for charitable organizations
- Industry events—national and local
- Other

ADVERTISING

> Advertising is based on one thing: happiness.
> —*Don Draper, fictional ad executive character of AMC's television series* Mad Men

Before you select an advertising method for your venture, take note if your business model is business-to-business (B2B) or business-to-consumer (B2C). You are the former; your customer (who pays you) is the latter. Marketing research has concluded that B2C business models respond to advertising significantly more favorably than B2B business models. If you think about it, this makes logical sense. Consumers are exposed more to advertising and the targeting reach is broader for consumer products than for industrial offerings. Marketing research has empirically proven this point. I hesitate to share the research results with you in an attempt to enable rather than limit your creative process as you select an advertising method. However, I share with you the results to keep you in the right ballpark. B2B prospective customers respond best to face-to-face selling while B2C prospective customers respond best to advertising. Advertising is third or fourth on the list of responsiveness in methods for B2B.

Advertising can be very expensive. Don't go nuts with your selections here if you are a start-up. Again, your advertising selection needs to be tested on a small scale first to assess the effectiveness in generating responses to preserve your limited resources. For example, if you select a print method in a trade magazine, think about running a one-eighth- or quarter-page ad before committing to a full-page ad. If you choose a banner ad on a high-traffic website related to your business model, I implore you to limit the size and timing of your ad initially to minimize your financial exposure until you get a sense of responsiveness and see the financial return on your advertising investment.

Advertising is arguably the most expensive, and consequently risky, part of the customer acquisition funnel. Recognize it as such and treat it as one ingredient in the customer acquisition recipe. My point is that your early investment in advertising (or any marketing method) must pay off now! You must find ways to advertise on a shoestring or risk needlessly losing your new venture's resources. Find an industry mentor or out-of-market competitor and ask what their most effective advertising methods have been. Why not learn from their experiences as opposed to your own life savings? This is part of the beauty of quality strategic business planning— to learn in simulation and testing before launching a full advertising campaign. Did you ever wonder why NASA tests everything in parallel, simulation, and testing before launching astronauts into space? We can learn from NASA and apply the methods of arguably the brightest people in the world—rocket scientists—to our business models.

Why shouldn't you test your sales, marketing, advertising, and PR methods before fully launching them?

Mental Exercise: Choose an Advertising Method

Take a read through the advertising methods menu following and choose a method you can afford that you believe will generate customer responses. Although you might be tempted to skip this section with a B2B business model, you will strengthen your customer target market funnel by eventually utilizing an effective method. You can record your results at the end of this module. Let's get creative . . .

Advertising Methods Menu

- Print: newspaper, magazine, newsletter, and so on
- Radio
- Television
- Outdoor signs
- Direct mail campaign—letter, flyer, postcard, etc.
- Electronic advertising:

  - Banner ads
  - Web links
  - Email campaigns
  - Blogs
  - SEO
  - Social media
  - PPC: click through
  - E-directory links
  - Cross-website links
  - E-newsletters
  - Web white papers
  - Web public relations
- Other

MARKETING

> In marketing I've seen only one strategy that can't miss—and that is to market to your best customers first, your best prospects second, and the rest of the world last.
>
> —*John Romero, director, designer, programmer, and developer in the video game industry. He is best known as a co-founder of id Software*

> The aim of marketing is to know and understand the customer so well, the product or service fits him and sells itself.
>
> —*Peter Drucker, Austrian-born American management consultant, educator, and author; inventor of the concept known as management by objectives*

Marketing certainly has changed over the last few business cycles, and it continues to evolve in new exciting, frustrating, and creative ways. The problem most of us have with marketing today is that we are so overwhelmed with all of the marketing messages that we receive every day. This marketing overload has also extended into our business lives. The Internet and social media have made this information overload even more numbing. What to do?

I do not claim to have the answer for you and your business model today. What I do know is that through a cost-effective marketing testing process, you can conservatively test various marketing methods to ultimately find the ones that will provide you with the greatest return on your marketing investment dollar. The reward at the end of this long and winding road is a set of marketing methods that you can turn on and off to fill or drain your customer sales funnel based on your needs, lifestyle objectives, or work capacities.

Don't get me wrong—this is far from easy. In fact, please do yourself a favor and assume the worst-case marketing scenario. From my experiences as an entrepreneur, instructor, and business advisor, most businesses or new offerings fail because of overly optimistic assumptions about the future success of the marketing methods they select. The kiss of death is assuming "instant-mashed-potato success" when it comes to marketing results. I cannot overemphasize this point enough to protect you. You will create the best possible value proposition and the best possible product or service you can. You will make your offering to the market, expecting nothing but success, and you will hear crickets, my friend, *silence*, no responses, ignoring your offerings on all levels. Just in case the visual is not as clear in your head as it is in mine, take a moment to intentionally hear the sound of crickets in your future as you test certain marketing methods.

Crickets, dammit, crickets! These fellows respond to ineffective marketing methods when no one else will. Did you hear the chirping cricket sounds? If you did, remember that this is what is most likely to happen to your early marketing methods, particularly if you do not test them first.

Let me wind down and share my personal marketing feelings with you before we select your marketing methods to test. I hate losing more than I love to win. I can have nine marketing successes in a row, and I will obsessively dwell on the 10th marketing event that failed, asking why it didn't work when I thought it should have. When I watch a client or an adult student entrepreneur fail at marketing on a new business initiative, it surfaces a pain within me that is difficult to articulate, but I feel it vicariously as if it were my own. Even after the client or student eventually succeeds, I beat myself up for not being able to help them discover the ultimately successful marketing method sooner. This is something with which I continue to struggle.

Promise me that you will go through this mental exercise, choose PR, advertising, marketing, and sales methods, and test them cost-effectively *first* before committing full resources to them. The ultimate success or failure of your new business initiative depends on it. Remember that "next-phase" or "second-phase" marketing and sales campaigns are axiomatically more difficult than the first or initial stage.

Mental Exercise: Choose a Marketing Method

Now it's time to select at least one marketing method that you intuitively or experientially believe will generate prospective customer sales leads for you for your second-stage sales campaign. Record it in the 10-minute Module 2 exercise on target market customers.

- Printed materials: brochure, catalog, business card, product sell sheets
- Electronic media: website, email, CD, Internet, video presentations, search engines
- Reference resources: directories, associations, phone books, lists, electronic, and nonelectronic
- Trade shows
- Direct mail: letter with collateral material, proposal writing
- Association activities
- Social networking
- Mobile marketing
- Networking
- Referral marketing
- Other

SALES

> In sales, a referral is the key to the door
> of resistance.
> —*Bo Bennett, founder of Adgrafix*

Before this writing, I read on average approximately 100 business plans in a typical year; after this writing,

I have a strange feeling that the volume is about to rise. I love them. I have the privilege of learning about the passions, personalities, strengths, and weaknesses of each innovator as I read. They represent the spirit of innovation in its truest form. During my training to teach strategic business planning at the Wharton Small Business Development Center years ago, Dr. M. Therese Flaherty insisted that I not ever judge a business model. She cited many examples of peculiar business models with poorly written plans that became industrial giants. That was some quality advice for a new instructor. I am careful not to judge any business model, and this has become less and less difficult for me over the years. What I focus on as I skim, read, and reread a business plan are the inherent critical assumptions within the business model, particularly for a start-up venture. This I do know: the energy, resources, and professional commitment to selling the value proposition are more often than not understated in the majority of business plans, especially by the new entrepreneur. In the new-venture planning stage, the typical business plan I read tends to abdicate the selling process to someone else. Remember that it is highly unlikely that anyone is more passionate, convicted, or capable of selling your offering better than you in the early stages of your new offering. If you are new to entrepreneurship, make the commitment now to select sales methods with which you are most comfortable. Your success during these most vulnerable months and years depends on it. Take heart in knowing that some of the most successful CEOs that I know, who manage millions and millions of dollars, spend a portion of their time selling to clients in their own way. Veteran CEOs know from experience that the greatest impact they can have on their business is typically on the front end, to build the business they lead.

Selling has changed over the years. Businesspeople continue to resist sales. The opportunities to meet face-to-face and cultivate relationships seem to be diminishing over time. The paradox in business today is that we are people who need personal interactions to fulfill our inherent psychological needs. However, combine this need for human interaction in a business context, introduce the sales process, add an inherent resistance to sales, and conflicts form within us. Cherish any one-on-one, face-to-face opportunity you get in front of your potential customer to build a relationship. Due to the increasing pace of business in our time, and the simultaneous decrease in our perception of our time available, we are often left with electronic transactions, which can leave us extroverts feeling empty.

The good news about how selling has evolved is that there are sales methods available that your prospective customers are comfortable with. Few of us enjoy being "sold." Fewer still like to be "closed" during the sales process. However, when your offering is presented to prospective customers in a way that clearly fills a need or solves a problem, the customer acquisition (sale) becomes a natural step in the relationship as part of the natural business order. Your task is to find the most comfortable sales process for both you and your customers. Try not to force this rhythmic, natural business order, because the consequences are often negative.

Mental Exercise: Choose a Sales Method

The sales methods in the list following are self-explanatory. Choose a method that suits your personality, industry, business model, and customers. You might not know which method to choose, but it is time to make a decision on a sales method. You can try different methods. Record your mental selection at the end of this module.

What Are the Sales Methods I Can Choose for My Business?

- Personal selling: sell myself and my organization
- Hire a company salesperson: in-house, road warrior, or combination
- Independent manufacturer's representative—someone who sells on a commission percentage basis
- Electronic sales
- Telemarketing
- Trade shows
- Free product or service, work sample
- Other

Years ago, while I was being minted as a Wharton MBA studying marketing, I read about empirical marketing research, which concluded that it takes an average of 5 to 12 contacts/impressions/exposures collectively to convert a prospective customer to a paying customer. This is an average, but the findings have withstood the test of time. Some customers might require fewer than five contacts, while others will require more than 12, if you can digest that. Just know that after you build your funnel and create your plan of attack, you will need patience, resolve, and persistence to acquire customers. For start-up ventures it (generally) takes more time and more contacts, for obvious reasons.

WRITTEN EXERCISE PREPARATION

Select at least one PR, advertising, marketing, and sales method first for second-stage customers. Then generate a customer list for initial-stage customers. Remember your method selections. Gather your electronic address book, written address book, Rolodex, Palm Pilot, mobile phone, business card collection, telephone book, association membership directory, other directory, or any means you use to store business contacts. If you type slowly (like me), then you might want to handwrite your initial prospective customer list. Field-test results indicate that listing names of people or organizations works best and enables the innovator to exceed expectations. One field tester asked me to remind you that your customer is the one you invoice and the one who makes payment, not necessarily the end user of your product or service offering. This is an important distinction to note as you prepare your target market customer list.

CUSTOMER TARGET MARKET EXERCISE: METHODS AND LISTS

Take one minute to record your PR, advertising, marketing, and sales methods in Figure 2.4.

Then, in nine minutes, write as many names and business names as you can. You can go back later and add addresses, email addresses, and phone numbers for your contacts. After nine minutes, you should have a minimum of 5 and a maximum of 90. Believe it or not, there are people who can actually whip through an electronic address book and record a contact name every six seconds to reach 90 names. If you have a management team, have all members list as many potential customers as they can and give the winner a prize. Have fun with this. Start your clock, put pencil to paper, and ready, set, go!

Customer Target Market Exercise

- Limit methods to space allotment.
- Customer lists—use extra space.

METHODS:

Public relations

Advertising

Marketing

Sales

List as many prospective customers by *name* as you can.

Figure 2.4   Methods

Competition is not only the basis of protection to the consumer, but is the incentive to progress.

—Herbert Hoover, 31st President of the United States

MODULE 3

Who Are Your Competitors? Competitive Positioning

Viewing Your Offering Through Your Customers' Eyes

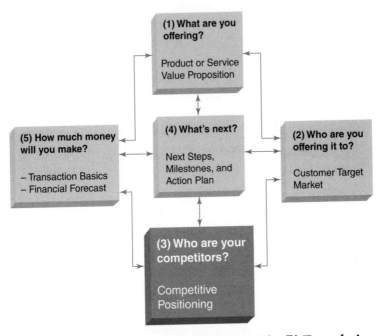

Figure 3.1   The One-Hour Business Plan™ Foundation
—Five Essential Business Plan Cornerstones

And while the law of competition may be
sometimes hard for the individual, it is best for
the race, because it ensures the survival of the
fittest in every department.
—*Andrew Carnegie, Scottish-American
industrialist and philanthropist*

> Competition helps people figure it out.
> —*Brian McBride, third highest all-time leading*
> *goal scorer for the United States national*
> *soccer team*

The competitive positioning module was chosen next because it is most closely linked with the customer target in the prospective customer's mind. (See Figure 3.1.) While you are pitching, presenting, or marketing your offer to prospective customers, they are making evaluations, creating opinions, and making final judgments about your offering. You are extremely fortunate if they are willing to share these thoughts with you. People learn from each other the way iron forms in a blacksmith's fire: with heated exchanges, repetitive pounding, refinement, a cooling-off period, and finishing. The symbol (not the logo) of the Wharton School of the University of Pennsylvania is the blacksmith's anvil, which symbolizes Joseph Wharton's pioneering work in the metal industry. I once owned a blacksmith shop that was more than 200 years old. While preserving the shop, I wondered what Joseph Wharton would say about the analogy of people learning from people or a blacksmith forming iron to the process of competitive positioning. Now that would be a seminar worth attending. Do you think we might earn some continuing education credits?

In this competition module, we will create a competitor table. A well-done competitor table succinctly portrays a value proposition offering relative to your competition in tabular form. The columns provide your top two competitors by name. The rows list the most important attributes of the value proposition offerings, as determined by the customer. A competitor table lays out the decision-making process of the customer among competitors. It forces you to be clear, brief, and concise and to resist the temptation to ramble on. A competitor table should get directly to the point. Frankly, I skim over most business plan industry-analysis sections and hunt for the competitor table to get inside the mind of the entrepreneur's prospective customer.

In preparation to complete your competitor table at the end of this module, avoid the pitfalls of "no competition" and of bashing your competitors. The second-biggest lie in the world is "I have no competition." If you are going to lie to yourself about competition, then at least list your competitive substitutes in the two columns in place of your two primary competitors. This will mitigate your pain when your prospective customers give you a headache after you go to market.

No competitor bashing, please. Write like an industry analyst if you can't write like your customer. Competitor bashing or disparaging the competition in front of your customers says more about you than it does your competition. It's akin to making a racial slur or a bigoted comment in a group setting. Who draws more criticism, the person who utters the slur or its target? You decide. If you still can't stop competitor bashing, remember that competitor disparagement is against the law in the United States.

"Okay, John, I don't have a headache, but I honestly do not know who my competitors are or how to find them." If this is you, then I can get you closer to your competitors, but you still have some thinking to do. We want to identify and analyze your competitive positioning before your customers do it for you and you lose them. For starters, I suggest identifying your North American Industry Classification System (NAICS) code and your Standard Industry Classification (SIC) code. You can find both on the NAICS Association's website at www.naics.com for free. Armed with your NAICS and SIC codes, you can use these codes to identify competitors in the arena in which you compete. If you cannot find a code close to your business model, then you will need another competitive intelligence source. A second source is the industry association serving the customers and competitors in the industry in which you compete. There is an industry association for most businesses. If a search engine does not identify your industry association, then try the Directory of Associations at www.directoryofassociations.com/directory. There are many other association directories on the Internet. A third quality source of competitive intelligence and competitor identification is networking with industry suppliers and competitors outside of your geographic or market area. Tell them your value proposition and your customer target market (Modules 1 and 2) and ask them to help you identify the competitors in your area. Be careful not to discount what they say unless you are certain the names identified are not competitors. Your goal is to identify your most direct competitors before offering your value proposition to prospective customers. It also helps you complete your competitor table.

As an instructor, I hesitate to provide examples in the learning environment. Learners tend to use them as a crutch or a paint-by-numbers guide when completing exercises. Learning examples can inhibit the innovative process and the creativity fundamentally inherent in entrepreneurship and its training. However, a framework is needed here to simplify what can be a complicated, fluid, and dynamic subject matter—competitive positioning. It's like a balance sheet, which accounts for your assets, liabilities, and equities at a given point in time—like taking a photograph of the financial health of your business. Figure 3.2 is a sample of the competitor table exercise for Module 3 to help you position your offering.

The late founder of McDonald's, Ray Kroc, once said, "If any of my competitors were drowning, I'd stick a hose in their mouth!" Would you like to compete against this guy? Mr. Kroc was a pioneer in the fast-food industry. As an entrepreneur and veteran salesperson, he understood the value of having a clear, distinctive, and replicable value proposition. He knew his customers very well and ate with them side by side to learn more. He believed in the value of competitive positioning long before he built his fast-food empire. Although I doubt that Mr. Kroc ever completed a blank competitor table on paper, I can tell from the economic history of McDonald's

Competitive Offering	Competitor #1	Competitor #2	Your Business
Value proposition			
Core products or services			
Value-added offering			
Geographic territory served			
Industries served			
Pricing strategy			
Other 1			
Other 2			

Figure 3.2   The Competitor Table

that he carried a mental version of a competitor table in his head, understood the rows better than anyone in his industry, and thrived on knocking out the columns. He continues to provide competitive inspiration for many entrepreneurs even to this day.

In the event that you find positioning your business against Ray Kroc's business is more intimidating than inspiring, consider that he competed in an era before the information age. The number of companies in industries collaborating, cooperating, and even sharing today fascinates me. In some industries, your competition can also be your customer. You might form an alliance to gain economies of scale and purchasing power that neither of you could achieve independently. Business research has shown us that open, and I mean truly open, information sharing can expand the industry pie, thereby creating larger slices for all. I need to move on now. I just heard a faucet turn on and felt a running hose heading toward my mouth.

At this point it might be helpful for us to use an example of a competitor table, and for you to read about a discussion I typically have with my clients who are entrepreneurs or students in strategic business planning. This example is hypothetical, to protect the innocent and for illustrative purposes. Let's say that you have had a lifelong passion for gardening and horticulture and want to open up a garden center, which you call Jayhawk Garden Center. You live in the heartland of the United States, in Overland Park, Kansas, southwest of Kansas City, Missouri. Your value proposition focuses on unique and distinctive nursery stock for area residents who have a desire for distinctive plants, shrubs, trees, and colorful flowers, preferably native to the area, hardy, and just plain different from what can be found at a chain-store garden center. You want to help your customers create gardens and potted plants that are different from their neighbors' gardens. Your goal is to provide a leisurely shopping experience for your customers so they will come to your store for a gardening event, linger in your café, and purchase some unique plants, trees, or shrubs. Your goal is to have your customers savor the shopping experience like they would in a garden center in England, as opposed to the typical rushed garden center shopping experience in the United States.

You have identified your competitors, Wildcat Garden Center and Home Depot, while driving within a 10-mile radius of your proposed location. After delivering your value proposition to 10 prospective customers before you open, you have identified the most important factors your potential customers consider when they purchase "green goods." You just completed the exercise at the end of Module 3 (Figure 3.2) and it looks something like what's shown in Figure 3.3.

COMPETITIVE POSITIONING TABLE EXERCISE

This exercise might be the most challenging one in terms of completion time. Admittedly, I am making some assumptions here: that you have identified your competitors, completed Modules 1 and 2, and are up for the challenge of writing as much as you can about your competitive positioning in 10 minutes or less. A well-done competitor table is a gorgeous part of a business plan. It captures the decision-making criteria for a customer target market and accounts for various value propositions competing for customer money. Another reason this part of a business plan is so special is that competitive positioning gets updated and referenced often—because

Competitive Offering	Wildcat Garden Center	Home Depot Garden Center Department	Jayhawk Garden Center
Market positioning of value proposition	One-stop shopping for all your garden center needs	Lowest prices for the most common mass-market plants and materials	Native, distinctive, and uncommon plants, trees, and shrubs
Geographic area server	5-mile radius of single location	10-mile radius of multiple locations	7-mile radius of single location with mobile outreach
Core product lines	Everything from plants to pots, chemicals, accessories, and more	Name-brand discounted flowers, nursery stock, garden tools, greenhouses, planters, water, and accessories	Locally grown green goods, flowers, plants, trees, and shrubs hardy for the area and premium accessories associated with them
Value-added services	Store-owned delivery, category event sales, private consultations	Installation, low-price sales, project how-to guides for do-it-yourselfers, e-commerce	Landscape architecture design, sourcing perfect plants, in-house delivery, installation, consultations, educational events
Customer target market pricing strategy	Loss leader for event sales; prices within 20% of Home Depot's for overlap; 45% gross margin pricing on all other products	Name brands at low prices	Premium price for a premium product to premium customers, 50% gross margin minimum
Native to the area plants	Some plants native	Most plants grown outside region but cover hardiness zone	Most plants locally grown or at least in hardiness zone
Coffee shop/café?	No	No	No

Figure 3.3 Jayhawk Garden Center

it has to. Competitive offerings change, your offering changes, new competitors enter your market, and all of this needs to be accounted for concisely. Furthermore, other functional disciplines of a business such as sales, marketing, operations, information management, finance, and human resources need to reference this to work in a consistent, integrated manner. The competitor table is a practical, useful, and pragmatic tool for quality strategic business planning.

My one piece of advice for you on competitive strategy is to differentiate yourself from your primary competitors as much as possible. Differentiating your business model relative to your competitors enables your business, by definition, to stand out from the crowd. Put your offering in your customers' minds while they make purchasing decisions. Do you look different enough? As you complete this exercise, don't quit; just complete as much of the competitor table as you can in the allotted time.

If Ray Kroc were completing his competitor table, I think he just might cheat a little bit. He would bring three administrative assistants into the room and have them record what he says in shorthand, give three competitor tables back to me in seven minutes, and take three steps closer to me—with the hose still running. Maybe we can keep learning from Ray Kroc here: pull your advisor, business partner, and/or significant other into the room and have them record what you say. Whether you choose to complete the table alone or with a group, let's get started. You're on the clock. Have some fun. Time to start the stopwatch and fill in the blanks. See Figure 3.4.

Competitive Offering	Competitor #1 (Type here)	Competitor #2 (Type here)	Your Business (Type here)
Value proposition			
Core products or services			
Value-added offering			
Customer geographic territory served			
Industries served			
Pricing strategy			
Other 1 (Type here)			
Other 2 … (Type here)			

Figure 3.4   Competitive Positioning Table

It's when ordinary people rise above the expectations and seize the opportunity that milestones truly are reached.

—*Mike Huckabee, American author, presidential candidate, and politician who served as the 44th Governor of Arkansas*

MODULE 4

What's Next? Next Steps

What Milestones and Action Plans Do for Your Business

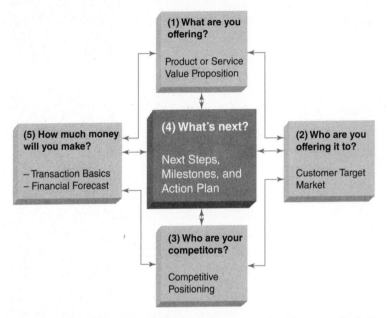

Figure 4.1 The One-Hour Business Plan™ Foundation —Five Essential Business Plan Cornerstones

My path has not been determined. I shall have more experiences and pass many more milestones.

—Agnetha Faltskog, Swedish recording artist of the pop group ABBA, one of the best-selling music groups in history

MILESTONE INTRODUCTION

I have an introductory story for you, which became a milestone after it occurred. (Refer to Figure 4.1.) The television network NBC10 Philadelphia hosted an event called *Small Business Week*. I was asked to come back to the studio to host an online chat room to wrap up the week. It was the Friday before Memorial Day weekend, and I thought to myself, how many people are going to be writing business plans late on a Friday afternoon before Memorial Day weekend? It sounded easy, so I agreed. When I arrived at the studio, I checked in with the producers, who told me that I would be in the main studio. I asked, "Why do I need to be in the main studio to host an online chat room about business plans?" They told me that anchor Tracy Davidson was going to interview me live on camera about business planning and that I would host the chat before and after the TV segment.

What would go through your mind at this moment? "How did I get here?" At first, I was a bit angry for being put in this situation unexpectedly, but I also felt flattered. I had enjoyed meeting Tracy earlier in the week—she was the embodiment of charisma, like an Oprah Winfrey for the Philadelphia five o'clock news. I thanked God I had worn a decent suit, looked at the producers, and asked, "What questions are going to be asked?" One of the producers responded. "I don't know." Respectfully, I replied, "Well then, find out—now!"

The questions came back: What is a business plan? What advice do you have for someone writing a business plan? While hosting the online chat, I thought, how can I summarize a subject matter I love, that is so encompassing and complex at times for people who have never been through the business planning process? This event forced me to just do it.

At 5:40 p.m., the studio manager's hand dropped, the cameraman's red light went on, and Tracy Davidson interviewed me live from a helicopter at the New Jersey shore. The horse I was riding hit full stride. It was an intense moment, but I did my best to explain that business planning is like a road map. It lays out the events and milestones that are most likely to occur as the business evolves. A good business plan provides a guide, like a road map, for you to reference when you need one. The best piece of advice about business planning that I could offer in 30 seconds, from all the business plans that I have seen succeed and fail, was to simply *talk to your customers first* before you write any business plan, because the business plan will be written very differently after you get feedback from your customers. After the red light went off, another TV reporter, who reported live in the segment before mine, walked right up to me and started asking me questions about a side business she was involved in. Whew! My father, who happened to watch the segment, told me that the cameraman made me look better live on TV than I do in person—thanks Dad (and cameraman). I regret not obtaining a copy of the segment for myriad reasons. Hey, I said that I am good at teaching this stuff and advising others to excel, not actually doing it well myself all the time. I want you to learn from my failures to minimize yours. Keep records of your milestones.

So what is a milestone?

Milestones have been around in various forms since ancient times. The first definition is "a stone functioning as a milepost." Milestones told travelers where they were and how long it might take them to get where they were going. Sound like a business plan? You may have seen a milestone while walking or driving a long road. Milestones take the form of stone blocks with numeric distance(s) sculpted on them or simply posts along a highway with distance points.

A kindred business spirit of mine at Farlex, best known for TheFreeDictionary.com, explains the second definition of a milestone: "An important event, as in a person's career, the history of a nation, or the advancement of knowledge in a field; a turning point."

If I asked you to think about and record the milestones in your personal life, what would they be? They might include your first love, your graduation from high school, your marriage, the birth of your child, your first home, your first gray hair, your divorce, the passing of a loved one, and so on. I hope the milestones in your personal life come to the forefront of your mind quite naturally and with more smiles than sighs. The milestones for your business might not flow as naturally from your mind, but they can be predicted before you get there, also, I hope, with more smiles than sighs.

Business schools teach us that milestones occur approximately every 90 days, or quarterly throughout the calendar year. They are normally broader than a goal and narrower than a mission statement. Milestones represent significant events in the life of a business. Business historians record milestones, ignoring the quarterly timing employed here in Module 4. Business historians write about business looking back from the present into the past. We, for business planning purposes, record milestones from the present looking forward, a much more challenging task. How can we possibly predict what our business will be doing 90 days from now, let alone one, three, or even five years from now? To prepare milestones we need to get ourselves comfortable with the ambiguity that forecasting inherently brings to the present. We need to get comfortable with the fact that we will be wrong to some degree of error.

It's easy to get comfortable separating what we can control from what we cannot. We can also get comfortable with setting milestones for ourselves in business. We need not know exactly when we will get there, but we want that milestone to happen, we *need* the milestone to happen, and we will identify and execute the activities that we can control to get us to our business milestone.

There is something very powerful about committing your milestones to writing and then working toward them. It is the energy, effort, and process that count on the journey toward a business milestone, more than the due date or measuring metric. The issue that we businesspeople have with forecasting milestones is often the necessary timing and quantification that we must place on them, which can make us literally wrong but figuratively correct. I do not pretend to fully understand this powerful phenomenon of putting your milestones (and goals) in writing and committing to them. The process of committing future milestones to writing is complex by definition, elevating the energy of human emotion, both positively and negatively. On the other hand, I do not care why the process works. I am an MBA, not a PhD. I know that it does work. I recognize the benefits of setting future milestones not just in my own business life, but also in the businesses of my clients and students. I want to share the journey with you here in Module 4 by enabling you to write milestones for yourself, reach your destination, and write new milestones again and again. Then you will have a sense of control over the future milestones you seek to experience on your business journey.

BUSINESS MILESTONE DEFINITION

To write a business milestone for the future, we need three elements: a significant business event, a deliverable date, and a measureable description of the business event. The significant business event typically takes the form of a series of goals to achieve. The deliverable date is normally expressed quarterly, but you can also set milestone periods of time such as semi-annual, annual, or multiyear. The measurable element of a future milestone enables either quantification or definitive determination, with a date in the future, and amply summarizes the series of objectives to prompt the business leader to monitor the milestone progress of an organization. Furthermore, the distinction between a business milestone in a strategic business planning process and a traditional milestone involves our view of time. We look forward into the future, not backward into the past.

Ironically, as I write this section, I am preparing a talk on business milestones for a group of business owners and CEOs later in the morning. These guys are smart, busy, competitive, and have shorter attention spans than a cat in a jungle. I have to get to the point quickly, clearly define a business milestone, provide classic examples, provide one specific example for each of them from what I know about their individual companies, and put them in a position to prepare better business milestones before lunch. It's a beautiful day. One of the visuals I will share with them today to summarize the essential elements of a business milestone follows in Figure 4.2.

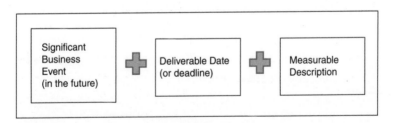

Figure 4.2 Essential Elements of a Business Milestone

ESSENTIAL ELEMENTS OF A BUSINESS MILESTONE

A future business milestone contains three fundamental components: a significant business event (in the future), a deliverable date (or deadline), and a measurable description. What significant events do you want your business to experience?

An assumption that I have about you, my reader, is that you are innovating something: a new product or service, an innovative division of an organization, or a new company. What are the milestone categories common to these innovators? Categorically, you can have milestones for the product or service development process, business-funding milestones, sales and marketing milestones, revenue milestones, employee milestones, operations milestones, and financial management milestones, to name a few. A veteran project manager can go on and on here. The point about milestone categories is that you can oversee and guide a business directly or remotely by categorically using a milestone management process.

What are some classic milestones in business? Here is a partial list of milestone classics:

- Completing the product or service prototype for customer testing.

- Hiring the first employee.

- Obtaining the first sales order.

- Receiving your first customer check or payment (some people even frame them).

- Achieving your break-even sales revenue level.

- Paying yourself for the first time!

- Leasing or buying your facility for operations.

- Paying off a loan.

- Paying back your investors.

EXAMPLES OF BUSINESS MILESTONES

This example (Figure 4.3) portrays milestones categorically by product, operations, marketing and sales, funding, and revenue for Your Company, LLC. Note that milestones are expressed quarterly here for most functional disciplines of business within an organization. The milestones themselves define something measurable without necessarily having to quantify them. This usually gets my clients and students going enough to apply milestones for their own businesses in the future.

Examples of Fun Business Milestones

- The birthdate of your new organization

- Having an open-house party for your customers

- Receiving the first payment for a new product or service

- Forming a business partnership with a person or entity

Your Company, LLC

Product or Service Milestones	By Mar 31, XXX1	By Jun 30, XXX1	By Sep 30, XXX1	By Dec 31, XXX1	By Dec 31, XXX2
1 Complete initial product or service prototype	X				
2 Complete beta customer tests		X			
3 Finalize product or service offering			X		
Operating Plan Milestones					
4 Lease initial facility	X				
5 Hire operations employee			X		
6 Install current management information system		X			
Marketing & Sales Milestones					
7 Finish e-commerce component of website	X				
8 Obtain first sales order for new product or service		X			
9 Hire outside sales person			X		
10 Begin field tested marketing campaign			X		
Funding Milestones ($350,000 total funding)					
11 Invest personal initial funds	$50,000				
12 Obtain fixed rate working capital loan		$150,000			
13 Complete investor funding round			$150,000		
Revenue Milestones					
14 First sale from new venture	$495				
15 Breakeven sales level				$270,000	
16 Profitable sales objective year 2					$340,000

Figure 4.3   Sample Business Milestones

- Displaying your company name, logo, and offering at an industry event

- A business retreat with your management team

- Seeing your name, company name, and offering in a print or electronic media publication

- Being recognized as a subject matter expert in your industry through a media interview

There are many others. I would like to know your fun business milestones.

MILESTONES IN PRACTICE: SANDBAGGING, OVERSTATEMENT, AND BALANCE

First, let me say that if you have investors or a loan officer, you need to be much more sensitive to committing to milestones than if you do not. Investors and/or a bank participating in the funding of your business will recognize the value of milestones in monitoring progress quickly (even if they don't fully understand what is involved). If your funding, through debt or equity, is dependent on milestone achievement, do you really want to commit to milestones that are a reach to achieve? If you do, then you will place yourself, your funding, and your business needlessly at risk. In the event that you are unfamiliar with the term, I would like to introduce you to an internal rival of mine named *Sandbag*.

Wikipedia defines sandbagging as "hiding the strength, skill, or difficulty of something or someone early in an engagement." Not that I am competitive or anything, but sandbagging has a negative connotation in most competitive arenas, because it understates a skill level to win a competition. In a business context, I cautiously suggest that sandbagging should be considered and even mildly employed at times as a milestone quality control check. Think about it. With the proper level of sandbagging built into your milestones, you can reduce uncertainty and myriad business risks. If your business funding depends on milestone achievement, then why wouldn't you understate the measurable to the highest degree you can without being detected? Be careful with this advice. You cannot be suspected as a sandbagger or you might lose some or all credibility when setting business milestones and subsequent goals. As the leader of a business, you do not want to have milestones handed to you with a demand that you achieve them. The fun is gone at that moment. That level of business engagement creates a downward spiral in business relationships where milestones are used as weapons against you. On the other hand, you do not want to create future business milestones that you cannot achieve, because they might also be used as weapons against you. Again, be careful and manage the ambiguity of sandbagging that I share with you. I hope my venture capital friends don't read this (or that they still speak with me after they do)!

Milestones for you and your management team, while arguably less strenuous, should still be quality controlled with sandbagging and overstatement checks to achieve equilibrium of both risk and certainty. Note that I intentionally omit the milestones that I have achieved as an entrepreneur, executive, advisor, instructor, and author. When I look back on my business milestones, I understand that I have learned more from my failures and struggles than I did from my achievements. Admittedly, I have worked with business milestones so wrong on so many levels that I am uniquely qualified to teach you how to forecast milestones more accurately. I have made the mistake of issuing milestones to my competent management team without involving them because they "came down from on high." I have also been on the receiving end of milestones without my input as a management team member that might as well have come right out of a comic book. In summary, let me say that as your business's leader, to achieve your milestones, you need to involve and solicit as much buy-in and input as you can from your board, your investors, and your management team. After what can be a tiring effort at times, you are in a better position to develop an action plan and begin your journey to achieve the business milestones that you established for yourself and your business. The fun is back.

The business milestone and action planning exercise at the end of Module 4 should subsequently be in your mind as you prepare your daily, weekly, and monthly activities to achieve your quarterly future business milestone goals. I offer up action planning as a business tool that works for me, but I accept that it is not for every business person. Before we work an action plan into strategic planning and milestones, let's first define the concepts and provide some quality control techniques to help you incorporate them into your business life.

ACTION PLAN AND GOALS DEFINED

Before we address an action plan we need to first define a goal that Wikipedia describes as "a desired result an animal, person, or a system envisions, plans, and commits to achieve—a personal or organizational desired end-point in some sort of assumed development. Many people endeavor to reach goals within a finite time by setting deadlines. It is roughly similar to purpose or aim, the anticipated result which guides reaction, or an end, which is an object, either a physical object or an abstract object, that has intrinsic value." Well said. You might be thinking that a goal sounds like a milestone, and you would be correct. There are more similarities between goals and milestones then there are differences. However, I find them confusing to businesspeople when the terms are used interchangeably. The following distinction focuses on creating a process that helps you achieve your desired outcomes most appropriately. In this light, a major distinction would be to separate a milestone from a goal in the context of time. My observations lead me to believe that businesspeople prefer to have milestones that are broader, larger, and more encompassing than a goal. Goals are portrayed here as action items within an action plan. It helps me to compare milestones and action plans to a staircase. Imagine a milestone at the top of the stairs, the action plan being the series of stairs, and the action items inside the action plan representing the stairs themselves. Time for a visual break.

Employing milestones and goals in this manner enables many successful strategic business planners to monitor milestone progress with a subservient action plan containing measurable action items as a way to manage milestone achievement. To add an additional dimension of time, a future milestone is more likely to be recorded as a significant historical milestone after it is achieved than a goal might be. Hopefully the distinction of timing and the broadness of perspective is enough to remember and move on.

Action Plan

A good plan violently executed now is better than a perfect plan executed next week.

—*George S. Patton, former General of the United States Army*

The definition of an action plan is not as standardized as other business terms, resulting in some ambiguity. Perhaps this stems from the wide range of uses an action plan addresses. The *Business Dictionary* sheds some light on the term, defining it as "a sequence of steps that must be taken, or activities that must be performed well, for a strategy to succeed." Any tools that can help me achieve my milestone warrant consideration by me—how about you? The second phase of the definition, while mostly correct, is just a bit incomplete, in my opinion. A quality action plan should also include a necessary activity, a person or entity responsible for the activity, a due date, and any resources necessary for completion.

MILESTONE QUALITY CONTROL CHECK: "STIFLEGOAL" AND "STIFLESTONE"

I am going to ask for a little literary latitude here, as I believe that I am making up two new words (or concepts) for you now that might later catalyze your goal achievement by employing a quality control check: "Stiflegoal" and "Stiflestone." A *stiflegoal* is an unrealistic goal that stifles the people or entities responsible for the goal's achievement with unrealistic requirements. Similarly, a *stiflestone* is an unrealistic milestone expressed in a future context that stifles the persons or entities responsible for its achievement with unrealistic requirements.

Imagine a CEO who walks into a conference room, looks at his management team members, and declares,

"Sales will grow by 50 percent during the next six months and each of you in this room is responsible for delivering this goal within the budget established last year." It is a goal and a future milestone by definition and meets the essential requirements of either a goal or milestone. It is good for the company, good for the CEO, and probably great for business stakeholders. On the other hand, also imagine the effect this goal has on the management team members in that conference room: the vice president of sales, the vice president of marketing, the chief operating officer (COO), the vice president of human resources, the chief financial officer (CFO), and whoever else has the pleasure of being on the receiving end of that mandate.

I offer these extreme terms to illustrate a problem you might have with a goal or milestone: it might be a stiflegoal or stiflestone. These labels are intended to be such—they raise a red flag and recognize the effects on the persons or entities responsible, stifling them, perhaps so quietly that the effect becomes difficult to detect.

Setting stiflegoals can be harmful to people. If the goal is not achieved, then it may lower self-esteem and force the person to question his or her own ability. Over time, a series of constant stiflegoals can lead to business gridlock, process bottlenecks, and in extreme cases, bankruptcy. Be aware that a stiflegoal need not "come down from on high." It might also come from you. The comic strip character Pogo, created by Walt Kelly, once said, "We have met the enemy and he is us."

I am advising you to avoid setting stiflegoals or stiflestones for yourself, then developing an action plan to achieve your milestone. Sometimes I unknowingly set stiflegoals or stiflestones for myself and my business and live with the subsequent effects; it can be haunting. The physical manifestation for me became high blood pressure at way too early an age. I am working on this and have made progress. Again, my intent is for you to learn from my mistakes so that you can avoid stiflegoals and stiflestones and achieve success with less stifling disappointment, in less time, and with minimal resources.

Few can argue about the benefits of quality goal-setting. Goals provide focus on activities necessary for achievement; they energize people to work together on common tasks; they encourage persistence, efficient utilization of resources, and careful timing, to name a few. Business schools are filled with research extolling the benefits of goals. What is comparatively under-researched is an inherent drawback of goal-setting, particularly in an innovative environment, when learning might become inhibited. Unintentionally, the goal achievement process may oversimplify focus on a deliverable, which can at times ignore exploring, understanding, or growing from the people involved. "Goals provide a sense of direction and purpose," Goldstein wrote in 1993.* Locke et al.

---

*I. Goldstein, *Training in Organizations: Needs Assessment, Development, & Evaluation* (Monterey, CA: Brooks-Cole, 1993), 96.

(1981)* examined the behavioral effects of goal-setting, concluding that, "Ninety percent of laboratory and field studies involving specific and challenging goals led to higher performance than easy or no goals." True, but don't forget about stiflegoals and their effects.

Milestone Quality Control Checks

- A significant measurable event
- A due date
- A person or entity responsible
- Accounts for resources required
- Likelihood of being a stiflestone for those responsible for achievement
- Other

MILESTONE AND ACTION PLANNING WORKSHEETS

Write one milestone that you want your business model to achieve within at least the next 90 days and at most up to three years. Then write an action plan to achieve that milestone with at least one action item. Field-testing

---

*Edwin A. Locke, Karyll N. Shaw, Lise M. Saari, and Gary P. Latham, "Goal Setting and Task Performance: 1969–1980," *Psychological Bulletin* (American Psychological Association) 90, no. 1 (1981): 125–152. doi:10.1037/0033-2909.90.1.125.

Milestone 1			
Measurable event description			Due Date
Action Plan for Milestone 1			
	Resources	Responsible	Due Date
Action #1			
Action #2			
Action #3			

Figure 4.4   Milestone 1

indicates that the first milestone and action item can be written in five minutes, while the second milestone and action plan can take less time. If you can complete one milestone and one action item in less than 10 minutes, begin the second milestone and the second corresponding

Milestone 2			
Measurable event description			Due Date
Action Plan for Milestone 2			
	Resources	Responsible	Due Date
Action #1			
Action #2			
Action #3			

Figure 4.5   Milestone 2

action plan to achieve it, also within the minimum time frame of 90 days to 3 years. If time permits, write a third milestone and action plan. You can always revisit your milestones, goals, and action plans later. (See Figures 4.4, 4.5, and 4.6.)

Milestone 3			
Measurable event description			**Due Date**
Action Plan for Milestone 3			
	Resources	**Responsible**	**Due Date**
Action #1			
Action #2			
Action #3			

Figure 4.6   Milestone 3

Today, the concept of business is to make money. Making money is the name of the business.

—Muhammad Yunus, Bangladeshi banker, economist and Nobel Peace Prize recipient; as a professor of economics, he developed the concepts of microcredit and microfinance.

MODULE 5

How Much Money Will You Make? The New Offering to Cash Mini-Budget

---

A Simple Way to Predict How Much Money You Will Likely Make

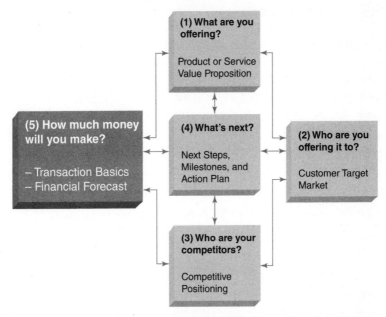

Figure 5.1 The One-Hour Business Plan™ Foundation —Five Critical Cornerstones to Build Any New Business Model

You're either making money or you're not.
If you're not making money get out
of the business.

*—Meredith Whitney, American banking analyst
and frequent contributor to CNBC, Fox Business,
and Bloomberg News programs*

HOW MUCH MONEY WILL YOUR BUSINESS MODEL MAKE?

The inclusion of the money module as one of the five cornerstones for the One-Hour Business Plan foundation was never in doubt. (See Figure 5.1.) The question was: Where to include it? When the inevitable time arrives to forecast money, it becomes quitting time for most people. They walk out of the room, leaving their plan where it lies, never to return, never to face one of the greatest enemies within them: fear. Fear of numbers—numerophobia! I am serious, my friend. It took me a long time not to take it personally as an instructor or advisor when businesspeople ran screaming out of the building and sprinted down the street, heading for the hills after their first attempt to forecast a profit and loss (P&L) statement.

That's why money is in Module 5. If you are going to quit now, at least you have four modules done and you're ready to go to market. I wrote this module, thought about it, and realized that it was too much for me to do in 10 minutes. The person without a business education launching a pottery business would have begun throwing pottery prototypes at me had I asked her to complete the original forecasting exercise. I had to simplify a forecast for the numerophobic, disassemble all the budget pieces, lock in on the most critical section, and ask my readers to complete only the most essential. Also, the miniature forecast I choose must integrate with the other four modules to maximize relevance and purpose for the innovator.

Then it hit me: recording the early customer financial transactions is the most important part of the budget process in the early stage of developing anything new. Without the customer financial transactions, we have nothing: no sustainable business model and ultimately no business after initial funding runs out.

To accommodate both the entrepreneur who works naturally and quickly with numbers and the numerophobic who eventually gets there, we address this module one step at a time, one transaction at a time, and in one sales cycle to predict revenue, Cost of Goods Sold (COGS), and gross profit. Module 5 is the longest, by design, to get you comfortable and then uncomfortable, to get you to achieve your mini-budget. We ignore most expenses for now, except for those that enable us to achieve the first customer transaction. After you achieve multiple customer transactions, you can manage expenses to gross profit and ultimately against net income after earning sales success in the marketplace. You need to take a higher-level look at the typical income statement budget and zoom in on recording those early customer financial transactions. View this mini-budget as a major cornerstone for your business model and see how it naturally folds into a more complete profit-and-loss budget. The Module 5 exercise is your mini-budget for now, which will help you create your more complete budget when it becomes necessary and appropriate to do so.

As a young math student, I ignored my teachers' pleas to set my math problems up properly. I just wanted to know what to do in my head, record the right answer, and move on. Perhaps you can relate to what I am writing about here. I got by. As I got older, the need to set problems up properly while solving them began to increase in importance.

Let me illustrate this point with a personal story. As an undergraduate student, I was taking a statistics exam when my calculator malfunctioned and my back-up calculator ran out of batteries. The professor did not have a calculator. All I could do at the time was set up all the problems and answer the questions—up to the stage where a calculator was needed. I checked and rechecked my thought processes on paper as I waited for the first person to finish the exam and then asked if I could borrow his calculator and return it at the next class. Thank goodness he was okay with it. I had about 10 minutes to complete both the calculations and the exam. The class stopped and looked at me. Two nursing students, both numerophobic, almost started crying for me in empathy.

As I was arriving late for the start of the next class, the exams were being returned. Some of my classmates started asking the professor how I did without a calculator for most of the exam. The professor told the class, "He got an A," and smiled. The class began to laugh and stare at me. Talk about embarrassing! The professor seized the moment to explain the importance of setting up a math problem completely and accurately before starting calculations and used my exam as an example for the class. Now that was a memorable quantitative event.

I share this story with you not to show off, although I will understand if you interpret it that way. My point is that I was forced to slow down and set up the best numerical answers that I could under extreme pressure. I checked and rechecked the logic and assumptions of the problems like I had never done before, because that was all I could control at the time until the calculator arrived. That experience taught me that I could perform quality control on my work *before* the calculations started. Once properly set up, the calculations were a matter of routine, and simply required concentration to minimize mistakes. This applies to the Module 5 money exercise, too, because we are going to take the time to set up our numbers (very few of them) properly. In fact, if we can get four basic numbers set up properly for you, the hardest part of the budget (forecasting revenue) should be a matter of routine. I had 10 minutes to complete my calculations, so I will later challenge you to have that same 10-minute experience in the Module 5 exercise.

Please accept my sincere apology for requesting that you complete a mini-budget in Module 5 in 10 minutes. My reason remains that the achievement of human potential comes when we are not fully resourced and are least comfortable. Our best achievements come when we are underresourced, strained, and compelled to achieve our best. Take heart in the fact that thinking and set-up time do not count toward the 10-minute requirement—only the writing time.

Before we begin, here is a list of financial terms that we need to define and briefly clarify to enable you to complete your mini-budget in the Module 5 exercise. I purposely chose to pull these definitions from industry, as opposed to academia, because I believe they will be more useful for you as you remember them in your business life. Take a read and enjoy the ride in tabular form in Figure 5.2.

You need to understand four basic financial concepts to complete your mini-budget in the Module 5 exercise. Forgive me if I am writing to you as if you were a fifth grader starting a lemonade stand. If you bear with me here, you should be more properly set up to complete your mini-budget. And away we go!

> We know, in other words, the general conditions in which what we call, somewhat misleadingly, an equilibrium will establish itself: but we never know what the particular prices or wages are which would exist if the market were to bring about such an equilibrium.
>
> —*Friedrich August von Hayek, Austrian, later British, economist and philosopher best known for his defense of classical liberalism*

Financial Term	Definition
Selling price	The price at which something is offered for sale.[1]
Cost of Goods Sold (COGS)	The direct costs attributable to the production of the goods sold by a company. This amount includes the cost of the materials used in creating the goods along with the direct labor costs used to produce the goods. It excludes indirect expenses such as distribution costs and sales force costs. COGS appears on the income statement and can be deducted from revenues to calculate a company's gross margin. Also referred to as *cost of sales*.[2]
Sales cycle time	(1) The time needed to take a qualified prospect to close. This means you have already found someone who has a genuine need. Now it's the time needed to "progress the deal" with all the relevant decision-makers in that company[3]; or (2) the course of time between the initial contact made with a customer, the identification of services or goods to be procured, the acceptance of the intended purchase, and the transaction that completes the sale. It is a measure of the efficiency of a sales department within an organization when compared with industry standards.[4]
Gross profit	A company's revenue minus its cost of goods sold. Gross profit is a company's residual profit after selling a product or service and deducting the cost associated with its production and sale. To calculate gross profit, examine the income statement, take the revenue, and subtract the cost of goods sold. Also called *gross margin* and *gross income*.[5]
Unit sale	A measure of the total sales that a firm earns in a given reporting period, as expressed on a per-unit of output basis.[6]
Month 0/Year 0	The month or year whereby no revenue is earned on the income statement; only expenses are incurred. A reference to "no revenue" in a time period of months or years for a stand-alone business unit with a separate income statement, typically associated with a separate start-up division or other stand-alone business entity.
Forecast	The act of predicting business activity for a future period of time. Typically, it is a projection based upon specific assumptions, such as targeted prospects or a defined sales strategy. For example, a sales pro forma in a business plan is considered a forecast.[7]

[1] thefreedictionary.com.
[2] investopedia.com.
[3] sales2.com.
[4] businessdictionary.com.
[5] investopedia.com.
[6] investopedia.com.
[7] businessdictionary.com.

Figure 5.2   Financial Terms Table

Financial Term	Definition
Income statement a/k/a profit and loss statement or P&L	A report that shows how much revenue a company earned over a specific time period (usually for a year or some portion of a year). An income statement also shows the costs and expenses associated with earning that revenue. The literal "bottom line" of the statement usually shows the company's net earnings or losses. This tells you how much the company earned or lost over the period.[8]
Budget	An estimate of costs, revenues, and resources over a specified period, reflecting a reading of future financial conditions and goals. One of the most important administrative tools, a budget serves also as a: (1) plan of action for achieving quantified objectives, (2) standard for measuring performance, and (3) device for coping with foreseeable adverse situations.[9]
Entrepretherapist	A mental health professional that provides therapy and psychological healing for entrepreneurs, particularly after failing to meet their budgets, especially if they have not prepared one or followed the advice in the One-Hour Business Plan Foundation. (Gotcha! Just seeing if you were paying attention.)

[8]sec.gov.
[9]businessdictionary.com.

Figure 5.2 *(continued)*

> Anybody can cut prices, but it takes brains to produce a better article.
>
> —*Ross Perot, American presidential candidate and founder of Electronic Data Systems*

SELLING PRICE

A selling price is basically the money that you receive for your offering that your customer is willing to pay. There are two fundamental methods to set your selling price other than making one up (although many do that well, not yet my friend). First, the market-based method, where you know what your competitors' (or competitive substitutes') selling prices are for similar offerings. You make an adjustment for your comparative value contribution up or down and set the price that your prospective customer is most likely to pay. Second, the mark-up method: establishing a selling price accounts for any and all known costs associated with delivering your offering. Make a note to focus on your direct versus indirect costs here. Then mark up or add the profit that you need to deliver the offering. At times, we can mathematically use the mark-up method of setting a price without accounting for the fair value exchange required by both parties to transact. Therefore, I suggest using both methods and setting the price that both you and your customer will most likely perceive as fair. Record the selling price for your new offering here:

> If we could sell our experiences for what they cost us, we'd all be millionaires.
> —*Abigail Van Buren, American advice columnist and radio show host who began the "Dear Abby" column*

Cost of goods sold (COGS): COGS is also known as *cost of sales* (COS), *unit cost*, or *bill of materials*. You have to love the English language at this moment. If you still need a handle on what COGS is, think simply about who you pay—your suppliers, subcontractors, and employees—to *directly* deliver your product or service offering. As an instructor, I find that some entrepreneurs struggle with quantifying their COGS, particularly those with a service offering. For entrepreneurs with a product offering, it is relatively easier. They simply estimate their material costs, *direct* labor costs, packaging costs, and inland freight, and they are done for now. For service-offering entrepreneurs, the backlash from forcing entrepreneurs to quantify their business model in terms of unit cost is challenging as an instructor. The resistance monster initially rears its ugly head. Yes, this might be you, my service provider. I have seen that look before and I feel it through these words from your skeptical eyes. "I don't have any direct costs; it's just me making the offering." Okay, if this is you, set your COGS at $0.00 for now and account for your expenses as indirect below, in the expense section of your income statement budget or P&L.

Before moving gently on to the next critical financial metric, at least think about what you are ultimately going to have to *directly* (there's that term again) pay your first employee, subcontractor, or supplier to deliver your service offering. To pedagogically push back, let me ask you a few questions, my service provider. Do you have any printed or electronic materials that you need to purchase to directly deliver your service offering? Do you have any training that you or your employees need to deliver the service offering for which you need to pay? Do you have to travel to your customer, who may or may not reimburse you via your customer invoice? I'll stop now. Just estimate and total your costs directly attributable to the service offering to your customer or just enter $0.00 for COGS.

What is your average COGS? Enter your estimate here and we move on to the next key forecasting metric.

> When you encounter difficulties and
> contradictions, do not try to break them,
> but bend them with gentleness and time.
> —*Saint Francis de Sales, Geneva Bishop and saint
> in the Roman Catholic Church, most noted for his
> gentle approach to the religious divisions resulting
> from the Protestant Reformation*

AVERAGE SALES CYCLE TIME/CUSTOMER ACQUISITION TIME

How many days will it take you to acquire your first customer? How many days will it take to acquire your second, third, tenth, or even hundredth? Did you complete the Module 2 exercise regarding your customer target market list? Now the numerophobic fear monster reveals its full ugly head. Its body is coming next. "I don't know how long it will take me to acquire my first or third customer, let alone my hundredth customer," you might say. I know that you do not know with 100 percent certainty the average sales cycle time, but I do know that for you to have a valuable and useful miniature business plan, then you will need to estimate and later refine your average sales cycle time as a key business model performance indicator. You need to start to understand your sales cycle time in a business planning simulation before you experience it in the marketplace. "Where can I find out?" you might ask me, as if the answer were in a book somewhere. Here are my suggestions to help you get unstuck.

Don't look for the answer in a book. Here, I usually suggest talking to salespeople and other business owners in your industry and asking them, "How long does it take you on average to sell your offering from the initial contact point until the customer invoice?" Salespeople inherently enjoy talking. They are used to getting rejected most of the time, and having someone approach *them* about what they do is a breath of fresh air. Just respect them as the professionals they are—and avoid questioning direct competitors in your geographic competitive arena, for obvious reasons. By the way, salespeople make outstanding entrepreneur candidates, because sales are comparatively more important than other functional business disciplines in the early years. Other business disciplines can be more easily hired, outsourced, or subcontracted. Plus, an oversupply of high-margin sales provides a great financial "deodorant" for evolving business models.

Business owners are also a quality source for average sales cycle time. Think about it for a moment. They must decide whether to take less money home or invest that same money in marketing or advertising. They need to know how long it will take to convert that investment into a financial return or they lose money. They might not know the answer or even have heard of the term, because it might be something they do more than something they plan for. However, with the right questions, you should be able to get an estimated range from them. If you need to, talk to more people about their average sales cycle time; anyone else working on the front end of the business model rather than the back end should be helpful, although a well-integrated chief financial officer or company controller might have literal knowledge.

It took me a long time to learn to underpromise and overdeliver my goals, milestones, and business metrics, particularly with myself (still working on that one). For your first sales cycle time estimate, give yourself a break. Underpromise and overdeliver it now and record the average number of days here:

> I was long brought up to think that it was nothing short of a crime to miss a sale.
> —*James Cash Penney, American businessman and entrepreneur who founded the J.C. Penney stores*

UNIT SALES FORECAST

Now the fun starts in our virtual strategic business planning classroom. It's time to predict how many units of your offering you can sell in your average sales cycle time.

For simplicity, let's start with month one after we record month zero(s), for those of us with sales cycle times longer than one month. This is often where I lose the most entrepreneurs, in some cases for good. For some, the numerophobic fear monster starts to reveal itself in its full glory. If this is you, tame this demon by knowing that here you are only being asked to predict a business planning estimate of the approximate number of customers you can reasonably expect to acquire in one month's time. For some it is easy, for others more difficult. I focus now on the entrepreneur who finds this estimate challenging.

To help you answer this question, I have some prompts for you. How many customers can you approach in one month? Not comfortably or uncomfortably, but with a mild amount of pressure to challenge yourself as the best representative of your offering. By now you have a list of prospective customers from customer target Module 2. Looking at that list of prospective customers, which of them are most likely to buy from you in month one? After you start your PR, advertising, and marketing methods from the customer target market funnel, how long do you think it will take to invoice a prospective customer who has responded to your offering? How many of those can you close in one month's time?

These are critical questions, and they speak to the genesis of business model development. You can acquire first-stage customers on the sheer perseverance and will of your entrepreneurial drive in conjunction with a fair initial value exchange. Allow me to repeat that second-stage customers are inherently more difficult to acquire because they need to come from your PR, advertising, and marketing methods outlined in Module 2. You can achieve your first-stage customers from sheer will. Once you get through your second-stage customers and silence those damn crickets, then you are on your way, my friend. A business model is born. Get on that horse, feed it, nurture it, perform preventative maintenance, and enjoy the ride.

Estimating Unit Sales in Aruba

Before we complete your estimate, I have a story to share about estimating financial metrics. As I write this section, I am in Aruba on vacation. I went snorkeling today with the family near the capital of Aruba, Oranjestad. We chose Aruba Bob's Snorkeling (much to the chagrin of our hotel) after my wife performed competitive research online. Aruba Bob (real name Ken) got his snorkeling business started by simply picking up friends, family, acquaintances, and referrals for free, for fun, and because he had a passion for snorkeling (the work sample method). His first-stage customers came when he simply started charging for his pick-up, snorkeling, and return service. His second-stage customers came from referrals, blogs, and endorsements on Internet travel pages, which is how we found him. He delivered a memorable experience for my family. Our snorkel guides were Cat, who looked and swam like a mermaid, and Stewart, from the United Kingdom, who reminded me of a former rugby mate with a great sense of humor. Bob catered to my wife's every snorkeling issue before I could, to ensure that she had a great time. He took underwater pictures constantly and emailed them to us the same night.

If you are a numerophobic, skip this next section—don't even look at it—and jump to the Module 5 exercise. For the rest of you, just follow the logic and check my math to estimate the snorkeling unit sales estimate based on a few questions and observations, not a business assessment.

As I watch the sun crash into the Caribbean Sea, I realize that my entrepreneurial reader might learn from what I observed today about the business model development of Aruba Bob's snorkeling business, sales cycle time, and estimating unit sales, as a real-life example. Although you might think that I need help relaxing on vacation, note that Bob actually volunteered his business history while driving us back to our hotel. I was impressed by his ability to set up his second-stage customers as he literally delivers them back to their hotels. He is living his passion with his growing snorkeling business; he also runs a lawn care business back in Indiana during the off-season. Naturally, I asked myself, "What is Aruba Bob's sales cycle time in days?" Without asking Bob or his management team, I wondered what his average monthly unit sales would be, so I decided to estimate his average monthly unit sales from my observations. His unit sale forecast by month is calculated by 2.25 trips per day (the .25 includes night snorkeling) and two vans seating five people each on average. An estimate of his average number of snorkeling units per month can be made after a few observations and assumptions. Given an average of 30 days per month, the calculation could be as follows: (30 days * 2.25 snorkeling events per day; the 0.25 is added to account for night snorkeling) * 1.25 vans (the second van breaks down a lot) * five people per van * 65 percent capacity (few businesses operate at full capacity all the time), yielding 274 average snorkeling unit sales per month. For simplicity, this calculation intentionally ignores seasonality.

Perhaps I should skip this literal example and just ask Aruba Bob or his management team members about his average unit sales per month. Where's the fun in that? Aruba Bob was excited to be included in this book until I shared with him my estimate of his average monthly unit sales. The email exchange came to a grinding halt. I am too close for his comfort, I am way off base, or he is just having too much fun snorkeling in Aruba to respond to me.

You don't have to follow a quantitative method of estimating your month-one unit sales as outlined in the snorkeling unit sales estimated above. You can qualitatively estimate how many customers you can acquire in one month from your customer target market list in Module 2. Don't concern yourself with being right or wrong for now. Just get started on your new offering business journey by estimating your first month's unit sales here:

Congratulations! You have just completed the necessary inputs for forecasting month one's gross profit dollars. All we have to do is provide some sense of structure and repetition for the Module 5 exercise unit sales estimate.

> A budget tells us what we can't afford, but it doesn't keep us from buying it.
> —*William Feather, American publisher, author, and founder of* William Feather Magazine

THE NEW OFFERING TO CASH MINI-BUDGET WORKSHEET EXERCISE

You are ready. First, deduct one minute, calculated with four numbers at 15 seconds, for your earlier written preparation. You have nine minutes. All I am asking you to do here, after you set your timer for nine minutes, is:

- Transfer to Figure 5.3 the four numbers from the earlier boxes: selling price, COGS, average sales cycle time, and unit sales for month 1 (after month[s] 0).

- Look at the average sales cycle time and estimate unit sales for month 2 and month 3.

  (Do no calculations here; you are simply setting up the money problem for now. There will be time for calculations later.)

- Estimate the sales and marketing money you will have to spend to acquire your initial customers for your new offering from Module 2.

- Focus!

Assumption Metrics:					
Selling Price (SP), Offering 1	$—				
Cost of Goods Sold (COGS), Offering 1	$—.				
Average Sales Cycle Time (in months)					
	Month 0	Month 1	Month 2	Month 3	Total
Unit Sales, Offering 1	0				
Total Sales (SP * Unit Sales), Offering 1					
COGS, Offering 1					
Gross Profit (SP – COGS), Offering 1					
Expenses:					
Public Relations					
Advertising					
Marketing					
Sales Commissions					
Graphic Design					
Office Supplies					
Travel					
Website					
Postage					
Telephone					
Shipping					
Other 1					
Other 2					
Other 3					
Total Expenses					
Profit (or Loss)					

Figure 5.3 Profit and Loss Forecast via the "New Offering to Cash Mini-Budget" Method

New Offering to Cash Mini-Budget Quality Control Checks

After completing your new offering to cash mini-budget, here are some questions to ask yourself as a form of internal quality control. The effect of the answers should produce a budget that more closely forecasts the early financial transactions of your offering.

- Have you accounted for your sales cycle time and month(s) in your unit sales?

- Have you considered stage-one and stage-two customers as they relate to unit sales?

- What is the least amount of money that you need to spend to acquire your early customers?

- Have you overstated any go-to-market (GTM) expenses in acquiring your stage-one customers?

- How do you feel about your unit sales estimate? Comfortable, slightly uncomfortable, or stifled?

- Do you know what estimates you need to obtain in COGS or GTM expenses?

- Other

Now that you know what to do next to make this new offering to cash mini-budget come alive in your business model, consider building this forecast iteratively (multiple revisions) and incrementally (in sequential stages) until it's complete. Here you revealed the key metric inputs for your business model. Then you showed your sales and gross profit for your new offering for your first customer transaction. Subsequently, you have already captured your go-to-market expenses. Although you have not done your calculations yet, you have set up the initial answer to the problem of "How much money will I make?" Whew! Try to take a break and digest what you just did.

It takes as much energy to wish as it does
to plan.

—*Eleanor Roosevelt, longest-serving First Lady
of the United States*

Conclusion: Pulling It All Together

Using Your One-Hour Business Plan to Earn Customers Today

The final 10 minutes of your One-Hour Business Plan foundation (1HRBPf) are intended to pull together your five worksheets in a way that works best for you to go to market and acquire your first customers. Here we review the five cornerstones of the business plan foundation to help you integrate them into a working, living document. The importance of beta users (field testers) is emphasized next as well as additional thoughts to support the work.

To summarize the 1HRBPf, I observed patterns in 1,000-plus business plans, actively watched businesses start, became angry at watching people needlessly fail, and wrote this work for the benefit of future innovators. Few people can argue that writing a quality business plan is not good for business. It provides us with a road map to guide ourselves toward desired outcomes. However, writing a business plan is like going to the dentist for most people. It is very good for you, yet can be painful at times and at a minimum uncomfortable. First, let's have some fun with the business plan writing equals dental visit analogy. My favorite visual of a dentist (other than my dentist brother-in-law and my dental hygienist sister and their perfect teeth) is of Steve Martin playing a sadistic dentist in the movie *Little Shop of Horrors*. Bill Murray plays the role of the masochistic dental patient. If you are afraid of the dentist, then jump to the next paragraph. Steve Martin begins with a display of the most painful looking dental tools in history, which strangely excites the orally masochistic Bill Murray. After the dental procedures, Murray responds, "Ooohhh, I'm going to tell each and every one of my friends about you!" Martin becomes so frustrated trying to inflict pain on Murray because he enjoys the pleasure of oral pain so much that he throws him out of his dental office and exhaustingly remarks, "Sicko!"

I might seem like Dentist Steve Martin to you because I enjoy business plans so much. Sorry. However, your oral health will be greatly improved by visiting your dentist regularly like your business health will improve by updating your business plan periodically. This minor investment in time both dentally and industrially yields abundant benefits such as minimization of future pain, achievement, and overall healthiness.

Now to the final 10 minutes of the the One-Hour Business Plan foundation. The five cornerstones of the 1HRBPf represent the five modules in this book. These five cornerstones embody a business plan foundation common in most successful business models:

1. Value proposition

2. Customer target market

3. Competitive positioning

4. Milestones and action planning

5. Money forecast

Five essential questions must be answered to provide a business model with a solid foundation. Graphically, the five cornerstones of a business plan foundation include what's shown in Figure C.1.

These cornerstones have a predetermined order necessary to enable a quality business plan foundation. The value proposition is the head cornerstone. An unclear or inarticulate value proposition subsequently makes the

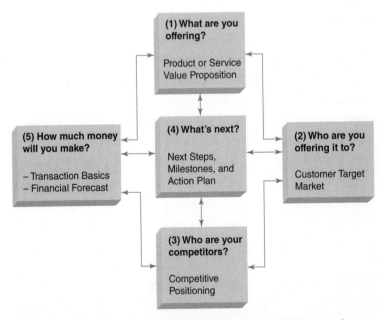

Figure C.1   The One-Hour Business Plan™ Foundation —Five Essential Business Plan Cornerstones

other cornerstones weaker. Innovators who skip the five elements of a quality value proposition often (but not always) fall into this category. Of the five elements of a quality value proposition, the customer's needs and benefits become paramount when creating a quality business model foundation. Let's be blunt. Most businesspeople don't care how you do what you do. Some don't even care what you do. What most businesspeople care about is what's in it for them. The "it" stems back to the needs and benefits transferred to the customer.

Cornerstone 2 represents the customer target market and the methods by which you will acquire customers. My entrepreneurial experiences indicate that you can get people to buy your offering through the force of will through people who know you, like you, and trust you. For those who don't know you, it's inherently more difficult to get them to buy. Second-stage customers and their adoption of innovations are inherently harder to acquire than first-stage customers, as described earlier in this work. The most difficult sale is to sell a new product to a new customer. On the flip side, selling an existing product to an existing customer is relatively easier. Module 2 attempts to teach you two things. First, the worksheet result identifies the specific customers that you plan to approach with your value proposition offering. Don't give me academic customer categories. I want real world names! Names of specific persons and companies that you believe today will most likely purchase what you are offering. Second, this module teaches you to choose the methods by which both you and your prospective customer are most comfortable doing business. These methods should be tested first with the anticipation of failure leading toward success. Given a valuable and symbiotic offering, money should ultimately exchange.

Cornerstone 3, the competitive positioning table, forces us to be empathetic with our customer even if we struggle with empathy due to our enthusiasm for our offering. Here, we get behind our customer and look back at both ourselves and our competitors from our customer's viewpoint. To properly assess our competition we must avoid lying to ourselves and concluding that we have no competition. Doing nothing or continuing with the status quo is your competition if competitors are unidentifiable by you. Trust me, you will find out who or what your competition is while selling your offering to customers. We strategically plan for that competitive buying experience through the competitive positioning table. The cool part about the competitor table is that it summarizes both our primary competitors and the most important factors of the buying decision from the customer's viewpoint, not ours.

Cornerstone 4 sets the business plan foundation into action through milestones and action planning. Far too many business plans sit on shelves disconnected from our daily business activities. Committing our milestones to writing from our mind to print enables us to see and monitor what we want to achieve in business. The action item activities that move us toward our milestone goals might change at times significantly. The point is to keep on keeping on and bridge the gaps among our daily activities, our action plans, and our work. If we can just put our electronic mail, telephones, and interruptions aside for minutes each week and monitor our progress toward our most desired business milestones, then we will achieve a more fulfilling business life.

Cornerstone 5 represents the economic purpose of any for-profit business, which is to make money. Here we work together on the customer transaction up rather than from a stifling revenue goal down to transactions. We work with the minimal essential numbers to forecast the profitability of any innovation: selling price, COGS, sales cycle time, unit sales, and go-to-market expenses. We don't have an unlimited budget for expenses, so we focus on only spending money that enables us to convert our offering to cash ASAP. To complete our money worksheet, we must ask ourselves a mission critical question about our innovation: "What is the minimal amount of money that I need to spend to facilitate the exchange of my offering for money from my customer?" Our worksheet focuses on the early revenue-generating transactions that empower our customers to fund our business model as opposed to loans or outside equity capital. Customer-funded business models are axiomatically stronger and more sustainable in the for-profit sector.

The final 10 minutes of the One-Hour Business Plan foundation are designed for stepping back from what you wrote and making decisions about what you need to work on most. This is difficult for me to write about or advise you on because each of us comes from different points of needs at different business times. As I write and look back on my day today, I advised both a vice chairman of a mid-size company and a postrevenue start-up company on their value propositions. The start-up has gone to market and received feedback from customers while the mid-size firm is refining its value proposition as it plans to acquire its customer target market niche. The value proposition is best refined after getting feedback from customers, not from listening to or reading my work. Just do it! I can definitively say that value proposition feedback from customers has refined and evolved more business models than any other entrepreneurial exercise that I have to date.

In *The 4-Hour Work Week*, Tim Ferriss teaches us that there is a major difference between prospective customers who say they like your offering and those who actually buy it. Nothing replaces receiving a sales order for a customer to substantiate the customer demand for your offering. Customer interviews and focus groups can be misleading and costly in time and money. Although I learned this lesson the hard way before reading Tim's first book, I want you to remember the distinction between a prospective customer liking your offering and actually placing an order for your offering. Be careful with the customer like versus the customer order distinction and don't forget to ask for the order.

The competitive positioning table is a quick and easy reference guide for your sales calls. Your sales calls will ultimately provide content for refining this table, particularly for those who think no competitors exist. The milestone and action planning worksheets look simple, but took years to evolve. On further review, perhaps your final 10 minutes of planning should focus on Modules 1 and 5. Then after testing your marketing methods, refine Module 2. For now, spend your final 10 minutes planning for whatever you feel that you need to work on the most and trust your instincts. (See Figure C.2.) You make the call.

You have just created your own One-Hour Business Plan foundation. Congratulations!

> Plans are nothing; planning is everything.
> —*Dwight D. Eisenhower, 34th President of the United States and five-star general in the United States Army*

---

1. Review your five cornerstone worksheets.

2. Prioritize what you need to work on next.

3. Combine your worksheets in order of priority.

Figure C.2   Pulling It All Together and Prioritization Exercise

I Love Beta Users of Innovations and You Should, Too

I delayed writing the conclusion of this work until the last minute, waiting for results from the beta users of the 1HRBPf. Beta users are testers of an innovation. Its origin stems back to International Business Machines (IBM) in the 1960s when IBM needed to test hardware and software products with end users of new technology. Today beta users are a special customer base to be cherished by innovators in any business in any industry. They provide us innovators with constructive feedback to refine our offering before we go to market more broadly. Take care of your beta users and they will take care of you. The beta users of this work will be specially rewarded by me.

A surprising benefit of working with beta users is that they teach us about their additional needs as they use our offering. Sometimes we have accounted for their needs and other times we must refine our offering to fulfill their needs. Beta users are most commonly utilized in software and e-commerce industries. Think about why. They have a technology-oriented innovation designed to deliver a beneficial user experience. Does it work? Can the user experience be improved? What results does the user seek? These answers are gifts for us innovators.

Unfortunately the beta users of the 1HRBPf are taking too long to report on statistically significant results. Business innovation takes time to evolve and I needed to publish this work for you. I wish that I could share with you the results that I am observing or the email that I receive. They might bring mist to your eyes. I can definitively conclude that beta user readers who engage in feedback sessions after each module are more likely to succeed with their business plan foundation than those who read the complete work and go to market unadvised. This advisory work does not have to come from me or my team, but it should transpire to support the innovator with knowledge, testing, and vicarious experiences in simulation. I can see that 1HRBPf users need to obtain feedback from a mentor as well as groups of innovators working on similar areas of their business. The collective mind of group constructive feedback is smarter than I ever will or can be and yields more positive results.

Failure in the 1HRBPf process shows up not so much after the entrepreneur goes to market, but mainly from an entrepreneur's unwillingness or inability to write. These people just keep on doing what they were already doing.

Success surfaces in many forms. Going through the 1HRBPf process and deciding not to pursue the innovation is in fact a form of success, not failure. Without the strategic business planning foundation process, the innovator may have wasted their life savings, years of time, or needless corporate resources. Well done. The other manifestations of success are obvious. An entrepreneur who makes a living by doing what she did in her job before she was laid off. An entrepreneur in the Pacific Northwest who quit his job to pursue his life's mission and is achieving his milestones. I can't be too specific without revealing confidences. Therefore, I have to move on for now and write about their results later. Ugh—I should have gone to journalism school rather than business school.

What are nontraditional forms of success in business planning? The immature entrepreneur might think, "Here's my great idea, where's my million dollars?" Go away. An entrepreneur who has been through a quality business planning process might conclude for himself, "Maybe I shouldn't pursue this self-employment idea, since on paper I can't make enough money." This will never make the media because it is not newsworthy, but it speaks to the preservative benefit of effective business planning—deciding not to proceed with the venture before significant money and time are wasted. Admittedly, I have helped new businesspeople become millionaires and increase their wealth, at times significantly. However, the majority of innovators simply gain clarity about how their great idea is likely to perform financially in the future. Getting back to the question about nontraditional forms of success in business planning, here are some more:

- Refine your business model—business models evolve after business planning.

- Learn the skill of strategic business planning to apply in the future.

- Complete a draft of a business plan—an achievement for many.

- Understand what you need to do during the next 90 days.

- Discover that you are not passionate about this particular business model.

- If you don't have time to write a business plan, then you don't have time to start a business. Why would any warrior go to battle without a plan?

- Discover that you have insufficiently saved enough money to launch.

- Know that you need to acquire particular industry skills and knowledge before initiating the venture.

- For existing business owners, you view your business differently.

CEOs AND ENTREPRENEURS HAVE A LOT IN COMMON

I wrote this book/program/course for the underdog, the disadvantaged, and the knowledge seeker. If this is you, know that I worked very hard to get this to you. However, CEOs with established companies seem to know how to use this work for their benefit more readily per beta results. As of this writing, I make most of my living working with business owners and CEOs, most often in the $10 to $50 million revenue range. These business owners and CEOs have similar struggles, fears, and problems that the start-up entrepreneur has when they innovate something new. They just seem to have a knack for getting through the 1HRBPf process more quickly and going to market and making money faster because they are better resourced and generally more experienced. In fact, I have one middle market client who has used the 1HRBPf process twice to create two new financially promising divisions and he hasn't even bought the book yet.

My point is that the CEO, business owner, and start-up entrepreneur share this in common from my viewpoint. They all:

- Struggle to articulate their value proposition of their innovation at some level.

- Overestimate the future results of their initial sales and marketing plans.

- Tell themselves the second biggest lie in the world: I have no competition. Please!?

- Are good at establishing future milestones, but understate the activities to achieve them.

- Have various levels of aversion to numbers, particularly in reconciling the money with the text in their business plan.

- Are humans subject to emotional decision making over logical decision making.

Planning is bringing the future into the present
so that you can do something about it now.
—*Alan Lakein, American author of* How to Get
Control of Your Time and Your Life, *which has
sold over 3 million copies*

OTHER APPLICATIONS OF THE ONE-HOUR BUSINESS PLAN

Admitting earlier that I love my beta users of the 1HRBPf, I committed to spending 15 minutes providing feedback after each module was complete and when they were finished with their plan foundation for free. For those within driving distance we often met in person. The questions and comments that I received during our dialogues caught me off guard. Here are three questions that surfaced multiple times:

1. "John, I know that I need a business plan, but what I really want is a job. Can this process help me with that?"

2. "This business planning process is finally working for me, but what I really want is a good man."

3. "I just moved to the area and need new friends (better relationships)."

Based on beta user feedback, I discovered that no matter how hard I try to make business planning simple for the majority of people, some will view me as a masochistic dentist like Steve Martin and tell me what they really want. Doesn't anyone want to write a business plan anymore? Alright, I give in. Forget that I spent seven years observing patterns, trends, and tendencies in business plans and venture initiation success and failure. My mission here is to provide the most essential components of a business plan foundation to increase the likelihood of venture success for you. It is working. Stepping back from the five plan foundation cornerstones, I can see this framework working in myriad applications. For example, let's take the job seeker for a ride through the 1HRBPf framework here:

1. Value proposition—What are you offering? What skill sets and experiences do you have that employers seek and will hire you for? List them, and then summarize them succinctly in sound bites.

2. Sales and marketing—How will you offer your skills and experiences to your employer (rather than customer) target market? List your methods, and then list the specific employers that you will approach.

3. Competitive positioning—You are competing for employment in a vast applicant pool in a great recession with a tight labor market. How will you position yourself to stand out with intrigue to your prospective employer relative to other job applicants? Complete the competitive positioning table accordingly.

4. Milestones and action planning—The milestones are obvious the action planning needs to change based on job-seeking activities leading toward employment. Keep refining your plan of attack and work it into your daily and weekly activities to land the job that you want.

5. How much money will you make—Salary or hourly wage is only part of the employment compensation package. Know what you need to make to break even and what you will be most comfortable making in terms of compensation. Don't forget lifestyle employment factors that often enable us to pursue our happiness beyond our paychecks.

Let's take the example of the woman seeking a good man using the 1HRBPf. Although they didn't teach me this at Wharton, it's kind of fun. Going through the framework:

1. Value proposition—What is it about you that you want to offer to a romantic partner to attract the most ideal suitor? Write inwardly about what you need. Then write in reverse about what this ideal man needs. Remember, women, that we are talking about real men here. If uncertain, get feedback from male friends.

2. Sales and marketing—If the telephone is not ringing and email, and texts are not flowing with date requests, then you need to do something to facilitate a relationship. What methods will you employ to offer yourself to your ideal male suitors? Online dating profile requests? Joining a dance club? Getting out in public where these men show up? You can literally advertise in a personal column, although that might

get scary. List your marketing methods and list your specific customer target market. Perhaps a male friend might make a quality candidate that you have not connected with in years. There's that feedback from prospective suitors of your offering again. Just make your list and keep refining it.

3. Competitive positioning—If you think for a moment that you are not competing with your sex for the best genetic makeup and men who can provide, then you do not live in the same world that I do. If you take some time to understand your female competitors, then you are in a better position to outflank them with careful planning. Don't forget the rows in the competitive table listing desirable attributes from your ideal real man's perspective rather than yours.

4. Milestones and action planning—Relationship milestones are obvious, but we need you to focus on the very short term here to facilitate relationship beginnings. While business milestones are expressed in 90-day increments, I suggest having at most monthly future milestones for relationship planning. The activities should be based on getting out in public and doing what you love to do in venues where your type of ideal man shows up. Try it.

5. How much money will I make—Alright, let's assume that you are not a gold digger seeking a

man to financially take care of you for the rest of your life while you live a life of leisure. One-sided relationships in business or romance have weak foundations and are inherently more vulnerable to termination. Why do some cultures offer a dowry to the male's extended family? Do you have an income expectation in mind? Do you know what the average household income is in your town? What do you bring to the financial table? A man with a reasonable understanding of economics can see the financial benefit of sharing expenses of home, groceries, child rearing, and so on. Although money might not be discussed between a man and a woman in a romantic relationship, it is often thought about. Why not plan for it?

I encourage you to write to me and share your "other application" of the 1HRBPf for the benefit of others. Wherever a plan foundation is needed, this work can:

- Negotiate a truce between two parties or even countries.

- Improve an existing relationship of any kind.

- Enable a more inspirational spiritual journey.

Just to name a few.

Although you might not have read this work to get a job or find a man, my point is that the additional applications of this offering came from testing this offering with beta users. If you test your offering with beta users, then new possibilities will become available to you that just might be more intriguing than your original offering. Try to be flexible and open to new and additional possibilities with your offering. An additional beatitude in the New Testament might say, "Blessed are the flexible, for they shall not get bent out of shape."

> We reinvent ourselves to solve a client's problem. It's more than just tweaking. It's rethinking what your audience wants and needs. Isn't that what great actors constantly do?
>
> —*Merrie Spaeth, American political and public relations consultant and actress*

ON THE ONE-HOUR BUSINESS PLAN CONCEPT—IS IT A GIMMICK?

Test results conclude that writing a business plan foundation in one hour is challenging for a new entrepreneur with no business experience. However, for those with business experience, particularly industry experience related to the innovation, writing a one-hour plan is being accomplished. Remember that I wrote this work out of frustration, watching people quit planning before they ever tried writing a business plan. So, I developed a framework in its simplest form that almost states the obvious. How can I inspire innovators to plan before they spend time and money? How can I get you to write at least part of a plan before going to market? I decided to make it a game. The game is called "Can You Write a Business Plan Foundation in One Hour?" When it's a game, people tend to take their mind off the pain and accept the challenge. We entrepreneurs are inherently competitive by nature. Competing against both yourself and the clock helps to articulate concepts, plans, and ideas from our head and into print where we can work with them more effectively in industry.

Another pattern I have observed with the beta users of the 1HRBPf is that those who go through the process for the first time do not complete the plan foundation in one hour; it's slightly longer. Most of those who go through the 1HRBPf process the second time do complete the process with time to spare. If you minimize your exposure to financial and time loss as a result of going through the 1HRBPf, do you really care if it takes you 75 minutes instead of 60 of writing time? The first time I used it, I got hung up on completing the competitor table. The other modules were completed in less than 10 minutes each. I have a client and business friend in Texas who in his late sixties started two businesses with this work in six months. The second time he went through the 1HRBPf he completed it faster than me and I created the process—very humbling. It reminds me of the time I ran a half marathon in Philadelphia and a woman in her seventies passed me. Okay, I can live with that. Then, a pregnant woman pushing a baby stroller passed me and I said to myself. "Alright, that's enough!" I needed to pick up the pace.

Plan your progress carefully; hour-by-hour,
day-by-day, month-by-month. Organized
activity and maintained enthusiasm are the
wellsprings of your power.
—*Paul J. Meyer, American founder of Success
Motivation Institute*

GET FEEDBACK ON YOUR PLAN FOUNDATION FROM ADVISORS, COLLEAGUES, AND MENTORS WITH SUCCESSFUL EXITS

I encourage you to submit your five worksheets to http://
planfoundations.com/trial. Unfortunately for the lurker,
you have to identify yourself and your business model.
I remember business models first, faces second, and names
third. It's the way that I am wired and how I roll. If all
of you submit business plan foundations for me to review
at once, then I am going to die. From my experience,
I know that a large percentage of businesspeople will
start, but never finish, their business plan. I can see some
of my beta users only completing the first two modules
and going to market, which is fine—just complete the
rest of your plan foundation as you go or later. Just do it!
Your business plan foundation and subsequent complete
business plan will save you time and money. In fact, good
planning can arguably make you more money the closer
that the plan itself resembles your core business activities.
In contrast, the more disconnected the business plan is
from the business activities, the less useful the plan is for
management.

Don't go at it alone unless that is how you know you best operate!

An obvious pattern that I am observing among 1HRBPf beta users is that those who obtain quality feedback from others are more likely to progress through the planning process, complete a plan, and move toward innovation milestones. I have publicly stated that you will receive free feedback on your business plan foundation. That commitment must be honored because it's part of what makes this business book a practitioners' business book more than an academic business book. You might have to be patient with the turnaround time. By the way, it does not have to be me or a member of my team. It can be your local small business development center, SCORE office, business group, mentor, partner, experienced friend, advisor, or better still three or more customers.

You probably know by now that I am a serial entrepreneur who struggles to limit the number of businesses I want to start. However, when I make the decision to proceed, I do some planning first (now with this framework) and seek out other entrepreneurs who have successfully done before what I am about to do. There is no better advisor or business education than that. Unfortunately, if your business is relatively new in economic history like electronic commerce, then there are not enough advisors to go around and they are difficult to find. Furthermore, an entrepreneur who has exited 10 years ago has missed two business cycles and might not be as current with advisory feedback as the entrepreneur and innovation require. If this is you, then you will need to find feedback and get advice from people who most closely resemble what you are innovating and from other business support systems.

I also see innovators in different states in the United States and English-speaking countries starting similar businesses. I need to connect these innovators (perhaps you) to work in groups and support one another, which is more powerful than working with one advisor. Ideally, you will be grouped with buddies/members/"partners" that are embarking on a similar journey. I can't do this for you unless you identify yourself and your business model at http://planfoundations.com/trial. The website is called plan foundations because people are using the framework to plan to achieve their dreams that have nothing to do with business. I will have more on that in some other writing because it is fascinating. I wish that I paid attention in English class now!

Furthermore, an additional pattern among users of the 1HRBPf is that those who obtain feedback in as little as 15 minutes between each of the five modules are more likely to complete their business plan foundation and become more enthusiastic about offering their value proposition to customers. This extends the writing time beyond one hour because the innovators are incorporating feedback and resubmitting worksheets with this incremental planning process. Note that I cannot afford to provide feedback between each module beyond my beta users unless I can find a way to automate the process and get experienced advisors to work for free or are funded by a third party. If you need this, let us know and we'll work something out that is fair and comfortable for all interested parties.

After you submit your business plan foundation to http://planfoundations.com/trial you will be entitled to a free trial period in a business club to determine if it is a good fit for you and for us. As promised, we need to at least get you some feedback on your business plan foundation. Here you are grouped with other innovators by industry, life cycle stage, plan stage, or whatever is needed most during the next milestone period. Eventually, we hope to provide access to a complete business plan series of modules for which there are approximately 15 essential components of any quality business plan. Based on experience and observations, I must insist that you complete your business plan foundation first and acquire some customers. Otherwise, the business planning process will not be as valuable for you. After all, successful strategic business planning is a journey, not a destination.

BENEFITS OF SENDING US YOUR WORKSHEETS

- Free brief but pointed feedback on your initial first draft

- A stronger business plan foundation based on feedback

- Free trial business club membership

  – Connect virtually with other businesspeople most similar to you

  – Tools and techniques that you can use based on business experience

  – Access to a virtual advisory board group of fellow club members

  – Other service provider opportunities, discounts, and cool business stuff

- Send worksheets to http://planfoundations.com/trial

> A good plan is like a road map: it shows the final destination and usually the best way to get there.
> —*H. Stanley Judd, American author of* Think Rich *and* California Weight Loss Program

HELP US GET THE WORD OUT—THIS WORKS!

I wrote this book/program/course out of the frustration of watching people spend their life savings, committing to years of debt, and wasting years of their time on an innovation that could have been tested in simulation with a plan. Why do people do this? Would you go into

Figure C.3   Getting the Word Out

battle without a plan? It is critical to get the word out (see Figure C.3). Perhaps the greatest value in this work is to predict how much money you will probably make if you decide to proceed with your innovation. Understanding how much money that you are likely to make can help you make more informed business decisions about your future and preserve your life savings. Although not newsworthy or sexy, it is preservative on a number of levels and ultimately a true form of success. If you knew that you were going to lose your life savings and waste years of your time on a business failure, would you rather know that through the strategic business planning process or from experience? That being said, many of you will innovate something new, create a job for yourself, and/or jobs for others. Some of you will perform very successfully. For these exceptional performers I realize that you will get to the point where you do not need me anymore. For the former, your successful failure is my successful failure, and for the latter, your success is my success.

For the reader who successfully fails or has success through the business plan foundation process, I hope that you will tell people about the 1HRBPf. Help us get the word out—this process works! For my readers who prefer not to identify themselves (and you know who you are) I am asking you to help me get this work in the hands of people who need it. Not so much for me, but for those in need of guidance and planning. Future innovators too far away from a major city or university often lack sufficient resources to help their businesses get started. These people in particular need your referral.

FINAL THOUGHTS

Eleanor Roosevelt once said that it takes as much energy to wish as it does to plan. People come to me in a dream state about their great idea. Their heads are literally in the clouds with their vision years into the future. It's what they originally think that strategic business planning is. Business planning looks into the future, but the primary focus needs to be on the next 90 days, the first 18 months, and maybe year two. My job is to return you to the present and meet you where you are. Metaphorically, it might feel like I am grabbing your ankles while your head is in the clouds and gently returning your feet to earth. Then we can plan in the present and explore strategic alternatives for your future. Together, we can help you make informed decisions about how to best utilize your gifts, money, and time.

Remember that you have completed a business plan foundation here, not a complete business plan. The word foundation was omitted from the title for commercial reasons. Don't forget to come back to your plan foundation and write your complete business plan after you have gone to market and exchanged money for your offering. If you follow this planning sequence then you will have a clearer vision, more detailed written guidance, and a permeation of planning throughout your business activities. Writing a complete business plan after transacting with customers is like looking at a comparatively more detailed road map while traveling lost. What a relief!

By now you may have noticed that I do not use the example method often when teaching business planning. I can give artists paint-by-number forms or I can give them a blank sheet of paper with guidelines and pedagogy evoking individual and innovative expression. If someone ever tells you that this is how everyone should write a business plan, the BS meter in your head should enter the red zone and a flag should go up. There is no one best way to do it for everyone. People have different learning styles, experiences, dreams, needs, and missions to fulfill in life. I have seen business plans less than 10 pages in length, outlines, slide decks, tape recordings, videos, and scratch pad notes with illegible handwriting build some of the most successful businesses in the United States. The common thread among all of them is the five cornerstones of a business plan foundation described here. It matters not how you express your plan foundation cornerstones, but it does matter that you record them, preferably for your stakeholders in writing. The power is not in the thinking, talking, or dreaming alone. The power is in the writing!

I understand that the writing is the hard part and I empathize with you. Therefore, the One-Hour Business Plan foundation process by design contains minimal writing time and maximum thinking time. Ten minutes of writing time after each of the five cornerstone modules plus the final 10 minutes bring it all together and prioritize your go-to-market activities. Come on now, you can do this! It only takes one hour if you organize your thoughts, focus your attention on the most important cornerstones, and build your business plan foundation and ultimately your business model. Break the habit of not writing by writing for 10 minutes after each module. Afterward, you will have broken through the barrier to quality strategic business planning by planning out your dream in writing. I hope that this is the beginning of our relationship and not the end. I wholeheartedly wish you the best in planning your future. Your innovation should be a fascinating and mostly predictable journey. Don't forget to share it.

Life is what happens to you while you're busy making other plans.
—*John Lennon, "Beautiful Boy." English musician, songwriter, and founding member of the Beatles*

ACKNOWLEDGMENTS

Kathy, without whom I would not be writing—and you would not be reading—this work.

Brian Borbely, for asking me for five modules, then receiving a book; for all of his success after Module 1; don't forget the other four modules sometime.

Sarah Hochburger, for the early inspiration, alignment, and focus.

Irene Lane, for helping me see what people want from me.

David A. Lancaster, one of the best friends a man can have and one damn good serial entrepreneur.

David Cantera, I never forget the first guy that says, "Sign me up, I'm in!"

Karen Lattanzio, Esq., for the early revisions and other applications.

The **Wharton Small Business Development Center adult student entrepreneurs, staff, Wharton students, and instructors**—it's been a privilege working with you guys!

NYC Business Solutions staff and clients, for the early webinars and in class sessions. Wow!

Lloyd Cambridge of NYC Business Solutions, for his service to budding entrepreneurs in New York City and their use of this work.

John S. Ondik, a great friend, fellow instructor, and a damn good strategic business advisor.

Jack Canfield, for a bit of guidance when I needed it most.

Steve Harrison of Bradley Communications, for helping me see the writer's journey so clearly.

Matthew Holt (John Wiley & Sons), for understanding what I was trying to accomplish for others with this work, faster than anyone to date.

David Drachman, for the publishing industry standards information.

Ricky Young of WHCR 90.3 FM, Harlem Radio, for his collaboration during the early version of the work and for encouraging his listeners to plan before they spend.

Tom Smith, for suggesting that I set the tone for my reader at Hello.

Andrea Cody, for being so successful with this work during the very first draft.

Lara "Ribbons" Zinda, for the early feedback and other applications.

Edwin (Ed) Price, for the exceptional encouragement, brainstorming, and brotherhood.

Buddy Steves, a gifted serial entrepreneur who knows how to use this work quickly and for making business fun.

Daniel Mainieri, Sr., for the graphic artist visioning throughout the work, regarding the five modules working together for the reader.

Rick Tashman, for the reader perspective, initial presentation, and friendship.

John Merriman, for the early national publicity and strategic positioning.

Jennifer Sherlock, for reminding me to stop and celebrate—and all of the fun events.

Fred Hawkins, for the ecommerce integration and reader life cycle adoption suggestions.

Art Finnel, for feedback on setting the stage for the New Offering to Cash Mini-Budget worksheet exercise.

Christine Perantoni, Esq. for insights about the book cover.

George H. Sullivan, author of *Not Built in a Day: Exploring the Architecture of Rome*. His approach to writing continues to inspire me.

The **Board**, for your exceptional guidance.

The **Beta Users of the One-Hour Business Plan foundation**, for your constructive feedback, entrepreneurial spirit, and for your successes in so many forms!

INDEX